CROSSING THE INVISIBLE BRIDGE

ISBN: [978-1-83663-963-3]

Printed in the United Kingdom.

ACKNOWLEDGEMENTS

Over the past 20 years of building global businesses by doing what I love, I've had the incredible privilege of learning from some of the world's most remarkable teachers and coaches. The powerful tools, strategies, and concepts you're about to discover aren't just theories—they're real-life lessons shaped by experience.

Some coaches helped me find the clarity I desperately needed; others guided me to become a better version of myself. Many mentors enhanced my health, fortified my mind and spirit, and helped me embrace life fully while discovering my true purpose.

I've invested over **$175,000** and hundreds of hours learning from amazing people like **Mac Attram, Grant Murrell, Tony Robbins, T. Harv Eker, Dr Andrew Huberman, Dr David Sinclair, Robert Spira, Dr Johnny Cortez, Dr David Snyder (NLP), Robert Kiyosaki**, and so many more. My mentors have been as diverse as military and law enforcement officers who taught me resilience and discipline, chess grandmasters and memory masters who sharpened my mind, incredible tango dancers who showed me the beauty of passion and movement, and inspiring strangers who touched my life in profound ways. Their insights didn't just help me succeed; they transformed me from the inside out. And now, I want to pass that gift on to you.

"Crossing the Invisible Bridge" is woven from the collective knowledge, experiences, wisdom, love, pain, successes, failures, and meaningful moments shared with these extraordinary individuals. Each encounter, each lesson, has been a stepping stone on this incredible journey.

Thank you, to all who have been part of this journey. Your guidance and support have made this possible, and I am eternally grateful.

DEDICATION

To everyone who still feels that spark within and refuses to let life just drift by—this book is for you. If you've forgotten how it feels to have your heart rumble with passion, let this be your reminder: it's never too late to reignite that fire.

I dedicate this book to my incredible and loving parents. They are living proof that hard work, dedication, patience, and love can grant your children a better future. They didn't earn much money, but they always provided everything we needed. They embody a generation of courage, integrity, and determination—values that stand in stark contrast to the haste of our times. Their example taught me that true wealth isn't measured by what's in your bank account but by the richness of your character and the love you share.

To my two wonderful girls, Malena and Grace—you teach me every day that true love comes in many forms. You give me the strength and motivation to prosper by doing what I love. My hope is to be the bridge that passes on the character and values of your grandparents' generation, giving you the tools and wisdom to thrive in our hectic world by following your own passions.

Remember, it's not about waiting for the "next time"—it's about making your next move.

Let's cross that invisible bridge together.

GETTING READY FOR THE JOURNEY

It was just before 3 a.m. at the Milonga in Salon Canning, Buenos Aires, when our eyes briefly met. She sat there, smiling. After many wonderful dances, a bottle of Malbec, and delicious empanadas, I was ready to call it a night. Still, I nodded to her with an inviting *cabeceo.*

Dancing with her was like moving through a forgotten era—a *tanda* (three tangos) to remember for a lifetime. When I walked her back to her table, I asked about the source of her boundless vitality. With a smile that carried the wisdom of ages, she told me:

"Young man, if you dance the tango and you don't feel your heart rumble, find something else to do with your time."

Her words haunted me. That night, I couldn't sleep. I couldn't remember the last time I did something that made my heart truly rumble when I accepted myself in such a beautiful way. That realization made me sad. I pondered my life's direction, realizing how much time and energy I had wasted on things that didn't make me happy. But no more, I decided. From now on, I will focus on things that make my heart happy and my bank account full.

Night after night, I returned to the Milonga—not seeking solace in the arms of seductive dances or at the bottom of a wine glass, but hoping to cross paths again with the 78-year-old lady who had gifted me life-changing wisdom in one brief encounter. Alas, our paths never crossed again.

Yet the essence of our tango moment stirred something within me and became the guiding light for my personal and professional growth. This journey led me to cultivate thriving multimillion-dollar businesses and empower entrepreneurs to realize their visions.

Though I've gained a wealth of experiences, whenever I recount the origins of my journey, my thoughts inevitably drift back to that *tanda* in Salon Canning—to a lady whose name I never knew but whose legacy remains engraved in my soul.

When was the last time you did something that made your heart rumble?

I wrote **Crossing the Invisible Bridge** to help people rediscover passion and build wealth doing what they love—principles I've followed for over 20 years that have changed my life.

When you take a bird's-eye view of your own life, you'll probably notice two things:

- First, you likely have a passion for something. It could be subtle or grand. Your passion might be anything from being a life coach, a personal trainer, a baker, a wine lover, a blogger—or just about anything else.
- Second, deep down, you probably dream of living a life where you turn your passion into a life-changing source of income and prosperity.

You're not alone in this.

But why, then, do most people fail to turn their passions into wealth and prosperity—even if they're masters at what they do?

- It's not because they haven't tried hard enough or because they aren't smart enough.
- Nor is it because they haven't read enough business books or taken enough courses.

If success were as simple as reading a stack of business books or taking professional courses—and then memorizing or repeating what others do—wouldn't more people be successful?

The truth is, when it comes to turning your passion into prosperity, you need a deeper understanding of the game of money. Simply mastering your art is not enough.

The strategies, tools, and ideas you're about to discover in this book will give you an unfair advantage that most people never get. You don't have to be an online marketing whiz or a business expert to benefit immensely from the wisdom here.

Crossing the Invisible Bridge is not a university textbook or a blueprint you should blindly follow. Instead, it's a practical guide to help you own and win your position with clarity and live the life you deserve.

A Scientific System—How to Benefit Most from This Book

The unique information in this book is deeply rooted in strategies developed by chess grandmasters, international memory experts, military strategists, and self-made millionaires. The clarity you'll gain over any position along your journey will put you in a place where, on your worst day, you'll find better moves than 97% of people on their best day.

Before you start your journey with this book, let me give you three techniques to boost the value you get from your investment:

- **Knowledge Integration System**: The book is designed, with input from international memory champions, to enhance memorization and integration of information. Each chapter with a key takeaway is accompanied by a simple, memory-ready illustration. This helps your brain associate the content you read with specific visuals.
- **Ideas Aggregation**: At the end of each chapter. Write down any ideas that come to mind as you read and immerse yourself in the chapter. Capture these thoughts as they arise—don't postpone realizations. Note ideas at the end of the last chapter of the book, "Your Personal Action List."
- **Action List**: Every chapter provides the opportunity for you to list actions you need to take. These are not just ideas but concrete moves you're planning to make. Taking action is the only way to grow and achieve your goals. Note actions in the last chapter of the book, "Your Personal Action List."

The ideas presented in this book are concisely organized with progressive difficulty, from the foundation up to the master level. As you go through the book, you'll feel excitement and enthusiasm building inside, and you'll want to run out and get started. This is how you know your journey has begun.

Ready to Cross Your Invisible Bridge?

Your heart is longing for more, **Don't let another day slip by.** Take action now and start your journey toward a life filled with passion, clarity, and prosperity.

Date	
Full name	
Commitment	I PROMISE TO READ THE ENTIRE BOOK AND FULLY EMBRACE THIS JOURNEY WITHIN ____ DAYS SO I CAN PROSPER BY DOING WHAT I LOVE
Signature	

CONTENTS

Part 2 – The practical tools, templates and cheat-sheets

Part 3 – The way forward and bonuses

"Most people fail to prosper doing what they love because they can't find their best next move due to a lack of clarity. They simply don't see the invisible bridge between where they are and where they want to be."

Ofer Valencio Akerman.

PART 1

The Game Changing Strategy And Your Personal Journey

CHAPTER 1

EMBRACE THE PERSON IN THE MIRROR

Your journey begins today, and from here, it is a life-changing one

She gazed into the mirror, whispering softly to herself:

"Next time, we'll do things differently. We'll laugh more. We'll love more. We'll waste less time merely working and start seeing the world. I've spent too much of my life staying quiet, working hard, trying to save some money. I was afraid, I guess. Keeping my head down, hustling just to get through life. Then one day, I looked up and wondered, how did I even get here?"

But here's the truth: There is no "next time"—only "next move."

Are you ready to make yours?

Stop Merely Existing—Start Thriving

Most people wake up every morning without realizing they're losing their game, day after day. They drift through life, letting others and external events define their priorities and consume their energy.

In fact, many wander through life reacting to things beyond their control. They stay trapped in a vicious cycle of living paycheck to paycheck, falsely believing their savings stand a chance against inflation, rising costs, and a system designed to keep them boxed in.

But if you're reading these lines, you're already one bridge ahead of most people. You've decided it's time to make a change—to prosper by doing what you love and live a happier, more fulfilling life. When you face the mirror, you want to see the reflection of the person you aspire to be, living the life you deserve.

You're about to embark on a journey that won't always be easy, but if you trust the process and follow through, it will change your life in ways you can't even imagine. Please consider the ideas presented in this chapter with every step you take along the way. And get ready to live your passion.

Things You Need to Know That No One Told You Before

Why do so many talented people struggle to build life-changing wealth, even when they're exceptional at what they do? You'll discover the answer as you progress through this book, but let's start with some powerful ideas to prepare you for the journey:

1) Personal Development Is Great but Not Enough

When it comes to winning the game of wealth, personal development alone isn't sufficient.

Many people engage in personal growth—they attend workshops, read self-help books, and follow motivational speakers. Others dive deep into business studies, learning every strategy that promises to make them millionaires. Yet they still find themselves trapped in the cycle of living paycheck to paycheck, unable to break free.

To truly prosper by doing what you love, you need to establish a balance between **Personal Development (PD)** and **Business Development (BD)**. But even more crucial is gaining the **clarity** that allows you to see and cross the invisible bridges and make the right moves.

2) The Most Significant Battle You Need to Win First

No matter how much money or how many resources you currently have, the principles of positional strategies you're about to learn will help you cross the invisible bridge from where you are today to where you want to be. The most significant battle you'll face is within your own mind. Once you master that, everything else will fall into place.

We'll delve into this framework in the upcoming chapters, exploring each element and how they intertwine to pave your path to success.

3) Big Things Don't Happen to Small People

From this day forward, every time you look in the mirror, remind yourself of this simple truth: **big things don't happen to small people**. As we progress on this journey, give yourself permission to be big—to attract amazing opportunities, to walk the path meant for you. If you're considering giving up on yourself, this isn't the journey for you. But if you're ready to embrace your potential, let's continue.

The person you currently see in the mirror might feel confined, or boxed in by circumstances, environment, friends, or even family. Yet the life you deserve and the wealth you can build are often outside of that box. The path to prosperity is filled with invisible bridges you'll need to cross. Along the way, you might realize that those who love you most may unintentionally try to keep you where you are, wanting to protect you or keep you close.

I remember a time when I felt exactly like the person in the mirror—confined, unsure, yearning for more. I was caught in a loop of working hard but feeling unfulfilled, wondering if this was all life had to offer.

After I decided to focus on things that made my heart happy, everything changed. I discovered the power of balancing personal growth with strategic positional thinking. I began to see the invisible bridges that had been there all along, just waiting for me to cross. This newfound clarity brought me power. That power made others see me as bigger—much bigger than I had ever seen myself.

And here's the amazing thing: **big people attract big opportunities**, and big opportunities lead to wealth and prosperity. By taking just a few steps in the right direction, I entered a positive ripple effect of growth, wealth, and fulfilment. I transformed not only my circumstances but also how I viewed myself and my potential.

I want to share these insights with you because I believe that you, too, can break free from limitations and step into a life where you truly prosper by doing what you love.

4) You Must Stay on the Journey to Achieve Your Goals

Over the years, I've developed many international endeavours, turning ideas into multimillion-dollar companies. I chose to open the book with a personal preparation chapter because of one critical factor: **you must stay on the journey to achieve your goals**. And this takes a lot of energy. So before we dive into practical strategies and tools, give yourself a chance to win. Forgive yourself for past mistakes and allow yourself to be bigger. Find your true purpose, because purpose leads to passion, and passion creates the energy to help you stay on the journey.

5) No Good Decision Is Made from a Bad Place

Feel good about the journey and yourself—no good decision is made from a bad place. Remember, your thoughts about yourself create emotions, and your emotions lead you to take actions that produce certain results. You can't win just by learning the business aspects; you must grow as a person to embrace upcoming opportunities and clarity. Take care of your health, nurture your emotions, and share happiness. You'll see how powerful this can be when done right.

6) Don't Ask Your Brain "Why"—It Will Come Up with Unhelpful Answers

How many times have you found yourself worrying about things that never happened, and by doing so, neglected the things you should have done? Our brain's primary function is to keep us alive, not to help us prosper. As we progress on this journey, stop asking your brain questions like "Why does this happen to me?" or "What if I fail?" or "But I don't have enough money...". Your brain will often provide unhelpful answers that won't aid your growth.

7) Become Your #1 Priority for the Journey

On this journey, you need to eliminate background noise. Distractions can be friendly, direct, open loops, intentional, or unintentional. Life and people will always demand your attention. But to complete the journey, you need to make it a **must-do**. Yes, many things are important, but you want more, and you don't have time to waste. Become your number one priority so you can complete the journey and help others do the same. Remember: **This is your game, and only you hold the power to win it.** I've packed this book with everything you need to succeed, but the next move is yours.

8) Invest in Learning

When I say invest, I mean truly invest—not just pay for learning. While learning is your best leverage, it won't help you gain a competitive edge unless you turn your learning into earning. You must use what you learn to improve your position as you go. I've seen too many people turn learning into an endless goal, accumulating knowledge without application.

On the journey to prosperity, learning must result in an immediate positional advantage. Ask yourself, **"How can I take what I've learned and use it to improve my position?"** Make this question a habit. When you develop this practice, your position will constantly improve, providing you with better opportunities and allowing you to make your best next move.

9) Ego Is a Killer

In the world of successful people, **EGO** can stand for **Eliminating Great Opportunity**. Don't let your ego define your journey. It can bring you to a position you can't win, exhausting your energy with high-emotion and low-intelligence moves. While you can use others' egos to establish your position, don't let your own ego get in the way.

Stay humble and focused on your goals. Recognize that learning from others, admitting mistakes, and being open to new ideas strengthen your position. Ego can blind you to opportunities and hinder your growth. By keeping your ego in check, you open yourself to greater possibilities and pave the way for lasting success.

10) Accept and Embrace Your Companion on the Journey

You have one companion who will always be with you on this journey. No, I'm not talking about the tax authorities! This companion is not a reflection of you; rather, it's a manifestation of all the things that make you uncertain, confused, stressed, fulfilled, and happy. In fact, it's a reflection of how you feel about yourself.

When you engage in any situation, people see and sense this companion—not just you. It's the embodiment of your inner state—your emotions, beliefs, and mindset. Accepting and embracing this companion means acknowledging your inner world and understanding how it influences your interactions and decisions.

I want you to keep this critical concept in mind throughout your journey. By embracing your inner self—both its strengths and vulnerabilities—you can navigate your path with greater authenticity and confidence.

You need to take care of your health to enjoy the journey.

Have you heard the expression "**Science always comes too late**"? Well, I have to disagree. It's all there, brought to us by leading scientists and doctors from around the world. I'm telling you this because I wasted so much of my life waiting for doctors to bring me scientific solutions for minor yet energy-consuming health issues. But it wasn't until I built a science-based health protocol that my life changed.

I've never been in better health, with more energy and a remarkable ability to focus—and I'm over 50 now. As a teenager in school, when all the kids ran the 2 km test, my teacher always shouted, "Akerman, we don't have a calendar here to time your run!" I miss my sports teacher; I'm not sure he misses me. Doing pull-ups was totally out of the question. I also had allergies, and every time someone sneezed, I caught a cold. Growing up, I just accepted this. When I started travelling the world for business, I always calculated two to three days to recover from the flight—so much downtime due to health challenges. My immune system was so weak. My eyes would be itchy and red, my stomach bloated, and every other night, I would get acid reflux.

Over the last ten years, I started following leading scientists, reading books on longevity, nutrition, and functional medicine, and together with advanced AI skills, I put together a health protocol that changed my life. Even during the COVID-19 pandemic, I didn't have a single sick day. My focus is stronger than ever, and I run 10 km two to three times a week for fun. Yes, I can also do ten pull-ups, and my energy is dancing.

As we embark on this exciting journey, I recommend that you focus on your health as well. Whatever you may be dealing with that consumes your time, money, and energy, I'm sure science already has a winning protocol for it. Don't wait for the government or even your own family doctor to bring the latest science to you—they can't keep up with the pace of innovation! It's your life, and we're going to make it even better—much better.

> You can access my personal protocols for free. See the book bonus (Chapter 15)

Yes, I Am 100% Committed to the Journey

Take a deep breath, look into the mirror, and see not just who you are now, but who you can be. The journey won't always be easy, but it will be worth it. Together, we'll gain clarity, celebrate the victories, and cross those invisible bridges to a life where you truly prosper by doing what you love—and happily embrace your partner, the person you see in the mirror.

In the next chapter, we're going to make a stark shift into positional thinking strategy and explore some practical tools you can instantly use to get your life-changing journey in motion.

Reflection notes

ACTIONS TO TAKE

-
-
-
-
-
-

IDEAS

-
-
-
-
-
-
-
-
-
-
-
-

ILLUSTRATION

Draw here the first visualization that comes to mind:

GRATITUDE

PERSONAL NOTES

Reflection notes

ACTIONS TO TAKE

-
-
-
-
-
-

IDEAS

-
-
-
-
-
-
-
-
-
-
-
-

ILLUSTRATION

Draw here the first visualization that comes to mind:

GRATITUDE

PERSONAL NOTES

Chapter 2

FIND YOUR NEXT "BEST MOVE" IN ANY SITUATION

Master your position, win your game

When reporters asked José Raúl Capablanca, the world chess champion from 1921 to 1927, how many moves ahead he calculates while playing, he replied:

"Only one, but it's always the right one."

Are you ready to find your next "best move" in any situation?

Let's delve deeper into this idea.

Do you know what separates a strong chess player from an average one?

Most people might say that strong players can calculate many moves ahead, or that they memorize more chess openings and best moves. But the real answer may surprise you.

What truly sets a strong chess player apart is **their superior understanding of the game**. This deep comprehension provides an essential framework for all their strategic and tactical ideas. It allows them to understand any given position better than the average player. In a very short amount of time, they can identify the best next move, putting them in a position to win time and time again.

Powerful, isn't it? So, how well do you understand your own wealth position?

Clarity Is Power; Calculating Too Much Creates Stress

I remember when I was learning chess strategy. I'd sit there, gazing at the board, trying to calculate every possible move, every threat, every quick win. The clock was ticking, and I felt the weight of each passing second. Stress consumed me as I struggled to see the next move, the path forward. The fear of making a mistake paralyzed me. My teacher stood over my shoulder, urging me, "Make a move! Make a move!" His words added to the mounting pressure, and more often than not, I lost my games on time.

It took me a long time to realize that I couldn't calculate everything. The endless possibilities and potential threats were overwhelming. I was trying to satisfy every scenario, to find the perfect move that would solve all problems at once. But this approach only led to exhaustion and frustration.

One day, after yet another defeat, my teacher sat me down and said, "You need to understand the position, not calculate every move. Find the move that improves your position, even if it's just a small step forward."

That was a turning point for me. I began to focus on gaining small advantages and improving my position incrementally rather than seeking immediate victory. With this shift in mindset, the game transformed. The stress diminished, and I found mental clarity. I wasn't overwhelmed by the need to satisfy everything or everyone. Instead, I concentrated on finding that little win forward and repeating the process.

This lesson extended beyond the chessboard. Life often feels like a complex game with countless variables, and trying to control every aspect can lead to a vicious cycle of stress and chaos. It can exhaust all your energy without getting you a single step forward.

Today, I use these skills to turn around businesses and resolve situations where people are overcalculating or blinded by emotions. I help them see that by understanding their position and making thoughtful moves, they can break free from paralysis and start making progress.

Far Is Scary; Fear Will Not Let You Win

Your destination can seem overwhelming—you can't get there by crossing one bridge.

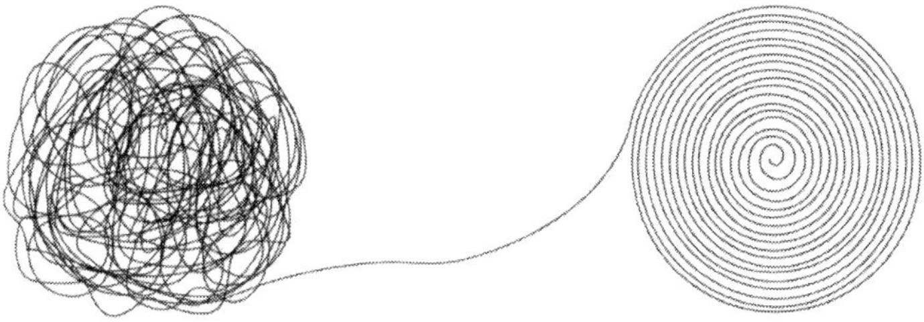

Calculating the entire path from where you are to where you want to be is an immense task—so immense that even the most powerful computer couldn't compute it. Remember: **Clarity is power, and chaos breeds stress.**

Most people fail to achieve what they want in life and business because they focus too much on the destination—the checkmate of their journey. They're eager to achieve their goals and improve themselves, often taking numerous personal growth courses and setting their minds firmly on where they want to be. However, the vast distance between their current position and their desired destination can be daunting.

Looking too far ahead makes it easy to become confused and lose sight of the immediate next steps needed to progress. When you fixate solely on the end goal, the path can seem invisible, causing stress and paralysis.

Consider a game of chess. When asked about the goal of chess, most people would say it's to checkmate your opponent. While that's true in the grand scheme, when you start the game, you can't deliver a checkmate in a single move. Instead, you develop your position in ways that will eventually allow you to checkmate your opponent. The best chess players focus on gaining positional advantage with every single move they make.

As you improve your position, more opportunities emerge. The horizon isn't as intimidating, your stress levels decrease, and you're already in motion—creating kinetic energy that propels you forward. With each step, your position strengthens.

Many people remain stuck in their current situation because the lack of clarity about the necessary steps to move forward creates stress and fear, making it difficult to break free. The main principle of positional thinking is that while you need clarity about where you want to be, it's equally important to focus on the **next best steps** you can take from where you are now, using the resources you have.

You can't reach your destination by crossing a single bridge. You need to find and cross the **smallest bridge that creates the greatest positional advantage** from where you are. A better position will provide you with more clarity and bring you closer to fulfilling your journey. Advancing in this way requires less energy and increases your odds of success at every step.

Positional Advantage Triumphs Over Material Advantage

Often, when I explain the strategy of positional thinking to students and entrepreneurs, they raise a common concern:

"We can't do it because we don't have enough money."

They tell me, *"We know where we want to be. We understand our mission and are fully committed to achieving our goals. But we lack the financial resources. How can we possibly succeed without money?"*

I want you to grasp a fundamental truth: **Money is energy, but it's not the only form of energy.** Unlike chess, where you're limited to a predefined set of pieces on the board, in life, you have the power to control and create your own position. You can convert anything you possess into momentum to propel yourself forward on your journey.

Here are some examples:

- Learning is energy.
- Skills are energy.
- Passion is energy.
- Clarity is power (and energy).
- Protocols to repeat small wins are ongoing powerhouses (and energy).

Progress is about incremental gains, not instant victories.

When people engage in any life or business situation, the one with more energy often wins. **More energy does not mean more money!**

There's another powerful element you can use to your advantage: the **pixel**.

When you look at the journey as a whole, the amount of energy you need is much higher. But what if you **pixelize** the next win? Improve your position by focusing your existing energy—including money—on achieving something small that grants you a positional advantage. Keep doing that until your position allows you the much bigger win. As you do this, you create a positive ripple effect that will take you much further than the direct impact of your energy investment.

There are endless numbers of pixels you can win along the way. Here are some practical examples of small wins you can achieve to improve your position (all explained in detail in the second part of this book):

- **Build a simple website** to showcase your ideas or services. Let it soak and gain ranking. Learn to dominate the niche online. It will grant you a massive advantage over your competitors.
- **Define and refine the value you provide.** Make it amazing.
- **Draft a basic marketing plan** to outline how you'll reach your audience.
- **Learn new skills,** such as digital marketing or networking strategies.
- **Refine your mission and boost your motivation,** solidifying your purpose and drive.
- **Learn how to use the power of AI to your advantage.**
- **Master copywriting** and make your message unbeatable.
- **Many more.**

By combining these elements, you move forward one step at a time. Avoid the trap of trying to make your first position your winning position. The amount of money you need to win the next pixel is considerably lower than what you'd need for the whole journey. And those little wins will change everything. The impact of the pixel is far greater than its size or the direct value you get from winning it. It's creating an energy change and setting you in motion.

Remember, everything is energy, and when people engage in any endeavour, the one with more energy—not necessarily more money—often wins. Even with minimal resources, you can initiate a sequence of pixel-sized wins and harness the indirect value these changes create.

It's not what's in your wallet; it's the pixels you conquer that will make you a winner. Turn it into a habit. Every day, ask yourself at the end of the day, **"Is my position better today than it was yesterday? And why?"**

Stop being a marionette in other people's plans.

If you don't own your position, someone else will—and they'll create narratives and strategies designed to achieve their goals, often at your expense. This is a critical turning point in your journey to success. When you lack control over your position, you're forced to react to others' moves. Reacting is a weak strategy. Operating within someone else's context means you're playing by their rules, within their plan, settings, and emotional state.

You must regain control of your position along the way. Be proactive. Set your own narrative and context. It doesn't matter how complex the situation seems—those who own their position always win.

"The skilful warrior puts himself into a position which makes defeat impossible."
Sun Tzu, *The Art of War*

It's not about the amount of money in your pocket or the resources at your disposal. It's about owning your position so you can find the best next move and continue progressing. As you gain control over your position and journey, your context—the environment you operate in—grows stronger, and you will appear more formidable and influential.

Especially if you don't have a significant material advantage, establishing a positional advantage is crucial to win. The power lies not only in the content of your actions but in the **context**—the environment and narrative—you create. Assess your advantages and disadvantages carefully. By owning your position, you tip the scales in your favour and set the stage for success.

The Power of Deflection

A deflection is a powerful tactic that forces an opposing piece away from a critical square or duty. In chess, this manoeuvre removes obstacles from your path, allowing you to achieve your strategic objectives. Often, progress is hindered because something or someone occupies a vital position that blocks your goal. By employing deflection, you can eliminate these barriers and clear the way forward.

SOURCE: CHESS.COM

For example, imagine you want to capture your opponent's queen without losing your own, but their king is protecting the queen. Directly attacking won't work because the king's defence is in the way. To overcome this, you use a deflection move to force the king to abandon its protective role. Once the king moves away, the queen is exposed, enabling you to execute your plan. The deflection isn't a direct assault but a strategic action designed to facilitate your ultimate goal.

Real-Life Example of Deflection in Personal Relationships

Imagine you have a close friend who, without intending to, is blocking your path toward achieving a significant goal. Perhaps you're trying to start a new business, adopt a healthier lifestyle, or pursue further education. Your friend, valuing your time together, frequently invites you to social events, late-night outings, or activities that consume the time and energy you need to focus on your goals.

Directly confronting your friend might strain the relationship, and declining every invitation could lead to feelings of guilt or misunderstanding. Instead, you can employ a deflection strategy:

- **Introduce Alternative Activities:** Suggest engaging in activities that align with your goals. For example, invite your friend to join you at a networking event, a seminar, or a fitness class. This way, you maintain the friendship while staying on track with your objectives.
- **Adjust Your Availability:** Schedule your most critical work during times when you're usually with your friend. By being less available for activities that distract you, you naturally reduce the obstacle without direct confrontation.
- **Encourage Mutual Growth:** Share your aspirations with your friends and involve them in your journey. They might become supportive allies rather than unintentional hindrances.

By thoughtfully redirecting the dynamics of your relationship, you remove the obstacle from your critical path without causing conflict. This deflection allows you to maintain your friendship while creating the space you need to advance toward your goals.

Winning the Joker Position

For years, I've carried a joker card in my wallet—a reminder of the lessons I've learned in the most challenging moments. This joker card came from the Paris Casino in Las Vegas, and while it might seem like a mere souvenir, it has become a symbol of something much greater. It taught me how to turn lost positions into success stories, and the secret lies in one simple truth: **a shift in perspective can change everything.**

The joker is considered the strongest card in a deck—powerful, unpredictable, and seemingly unbeatable. Winning against the joker can feel overwhelming. It looks solid and impossible to overcome.

But here's the thing: when you turn the card 90 degrees, you suddenly see it for what it truly is—a thin, fragile piece of paper. That small twist reveals a whole new reality. Just like the joker, many challenges in life and business are not as impossible as they appear at first glance. Any position that seems unwinnable must have a thin, fragile side. You just need to zoom out and give the position a little twist.

I use this idea often when turning around businesses. And it's also a great conversation opener. So, what do you have in your wallet?

Stay on Your Critical Path

The critical path is your way of achieving tactical advantages or even strategic goals. The path could change, but it should have a tangible target to achieve—something you can measure. One thing that may surprise you is the amount of energy you waste every day on things that do not help you advance along your critical path.

When you start your day, do you know what the mandatory things are that you want to achieve? What is the most important thing you must accomplish? You need to eliminate a lot of background noise—both direct and indirect—to fulfil your critical path.

Embrace Positional Understanding

Positional understanding separates the best chess players from the rest. It's not enough just to know the rules of the game or memorize some openings. Understanding the principles of creating and leveraging ongoing positional advantages will allow you to see and cross invisible bridges along your way, make better use of your time, and become more attractive to opportunities.

The impact is not only direct, and the advantage—like in the case of deflection—is not a result of the immediate move but a strategic gain.

Key Takeaways:

- **Focus on Understanding, Not Overcalculating:** Gain clarity about your position to make the next best move without being overwhelmed by possibilities.

- **Advance Through Incremental Gains:** Pixelize your journey by focusing on small wins that build momentum.

- **Own Your Position:** Take control of your narrative and context to set the stage for success.

- **Use Deflection Strategically:** Remove obstacles by redirecting energy and focus without direct confrontation.

- **Shift Your Perspective:** Small changes in how you view challenges can reveal new solutions.

- **Stay on Your Critical Path:** Prioritize actions that align with your primary goals, minimizing distractions.

By incorporating these principles, you're equipping yourself with the tools to navigate your journey effectively. Remember, the path to prosperity isn't about making one grand move but about consistently making the next best move. Master your position, and you'll win your game.

Reflection notes

ACTIONS TO TAKE

IDEAS

ILLUSTRATION

Draw here the first visualization that comes to mind:

GRATITUDE

PERSONAL NOTES

Reflection notes

ACTIONS TO TAKE

IDEAS

ILLUSTRATION

Draw here the first visualization that comes to mind:

GRATITUDE

PERSONAL NOTES

CHAPTER 3

A MEANINGFUL EVENING AT THE TAVERNA

The waiter that helped me live what I teach

That evening, I was convinced I was about to lose it all—my best friends, my money, my energy, and maybe even my family. I sat alone at a taverna, holding the joker card in my hand, letting the weight of failure settle in. It was just before the Jewish New Year, October 2nd, 2024, and I had come to Cyprus to try to rescue a crumbling partnership with close friends and business associates.

It all started a couple of years back when one of my best friends, Robert, a real estate mogul, offered me and a group of friends the chance to invest in a project in Cyprus. He personally guaranteed the money. I didn't hesitate for a second—when Robert was in, I was in. No questions asked. After all, he wasn't just a successful businessman; he was one of my closest friends.

But the project went off track. Tensions rose, and soon, fights began. Robert took his money and profit, leaving the rest of us—the buyers—stranded to deal with a disaster in a foreign country—or so we believed. The contractor suffered a major burnout and a nervous breakdown, disappearing from the picture. Emotions were running high, and it wasn't just about the money anymore. It was the betrayal, the shame—how could we have been so naïve? How could I, who had convinced friends and family to join, face them now? The thought of losing everything, especially my self-respect, crushed me.

That night, sitting in the taverna where I had once shared meals with my friends and partners, I felt completely alone. My mind raced with thoughts of failure.

But then, something unexpected happened.

The waiter, who had known me for years, approached with concern. "I've never seen you like this," he said gently. "Can I do something to help?"

"It's all good," I replied, trying to brush it off, and ordered some food.

A couple of glasses of wine later, I asked him, "What's with my food?"

He replied with a smile, "Listen, my friend, I finish here soon, and you're coming to dinner with my family. I'm not letting you stay here like this."

His kindness took me by surprise. It shifted something deep inside me. His compassion and generosity cracked through the darkness I had been drowning in, and suddenly, my perspective began to change. Instead of focusing on what I'd lost, I felt a spark of appreciation and gratitude.

The joker

After dinner with his family, he noticed me turning the joker card over in my hand and asked about its significance. I told him the story behind it—how the joker reminded me that what looks unbeatable might just need a slight shift in perspective. The next morning, every member of his family had their own joker card.

As I shared the story with them, the waiter leaned in and asked, "So why are you still so sad? How come you haven't turned the joker to see the next move?" His words hit me hard. In that moment, it became clear: I had been so focused on the loss of money, friends, and energy that I couldn't see the path forward. My mind was locked on the illusion of defeat, like staring at an unbeatable joker card head-on.

Turning the card

But now, with the clarity that comes from a shift in perspective, I knew what I had to do. It wasn't about fixing everything at once; it was about making the next move—a move that would reposition us to resolve the problem. I needed to bring the contractor, the investors, and everyone involved back to the table. It wasn't about solving the entire situation immediately—it was about setting the stage for progress, managing the situation rather than being managed by it.

Over time, anger had taken hold among the partners involved, but I used a deflection strategy to offer each person a perceived opportunity—to be the one who saved the project, to be the hero in the eyes of the buyers and investors. That meeting took place a few days later, and while it didn't solve everything, it was a step forward. We weren't in a perfect position, but we were in a better one, and that was enough to keep moving.

When you're facing your own "joker card" moments in life or business, remember that it's often about developing positional clarity. You don't need to defeat the obstacle all at once. Focus on understanding where you stand, what the people around you need, and how you can make a small, smart move that changes the dynamic. Sometimes, the most powerful shift comes from simply turning the joker and seeing the situation from a new angle—changing the context, not the content, of the situation.

The Dessert Menu and a Little Exercise

Sometimes, acts of compassion coming in totally unexpected ways can change everything. But you need to stay open to give and receive. Too many people go through life unnoticed, like faces in a busy train station. But this is a mistake. Like the story above, I've had many occasions where people I impacted—sometimes with a smile, a joke, a kind word, or a hug—appeared at the right place at the right time. Many of my greatest endeavours happened because I wasn't willing to go unnoticed. I strive to impact people around me in a meaningful way.

Don't be transparent. You have so much to offer. **Give, and you shall receive.**

Give it a try: For the next five days, as you go to the office or meet people, aim to impact three people each day. Make them smile, make them feel good about their day. Let them feel special. If you turn this into a habit, you'll sense a beautiful change in your life.

Key Takeaways:

- **A Shift in Perspective Can Change Everything:** Sometimes, all it takes is looking at a situation from a different angle to find a solution.
- **Small Moves Lead to Progress:** You don't have to solve everything at once. Focus on the next best move.
- **Acts of Kindness Have Profound Impact:** Both giving and receiving kindness can transform your outlook and open new paths.
- **Don't Isolate Yourself:** Being open to others can provide support and insights you might not find alone.
- **Make an Impact Daily:** By positively affecting those around you, you create a ripple effect that enhances your own life and opportunities.

Remember, challenges often seem unbeatable until we adjust our perspective and take that first step forward. Embrace the power of small moves, stay open to the unexpected kindness of others, and don't hesitate to be a source of positivity yourself. Your journey to prosperity and fulfilment is not a solitary one—you influence and are influenced by the people you encounter along the way.

Reflection notes

ACTIONS TO TAKE

IDEAS

ILLUSTRATION

Draw here the first visualization that comes to mind:

GRATITUDE

PERSONAL NOTES

Reflection notes

ACTIONS TO TAKE

-
-
-
-
-
-

IDEAS

-
-
-
-
-
-
-
-
-
-
-
-

ILLUSTRATION

Draw here the first visualization that comes to mind:

GRATITUDE

PERSONAL NOTES

CHAPTER 4

BECOME A POWERFUL MAGNET FOR OPPORTUNITIES

The best contract – on a napkin

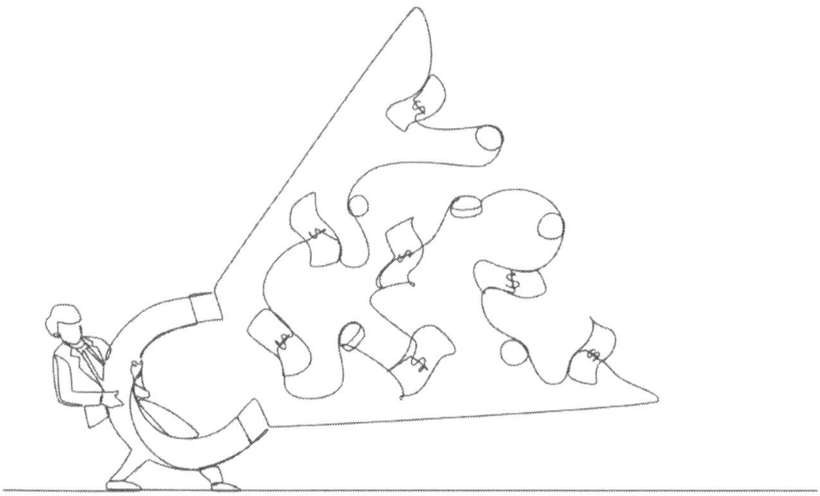

Have you ever wondered why some people seem to attract incredible opportunities while others, no matter how hard they work, struggle to move forward? The truth is that big opportunities come to those who are ready to receive them.

Small minds, limited beliefs, and a lack of preparation push away the very success you desire. If you want to attract world-class opportunities, you must elevate yourself to a level where you not only recognize them but are fully prepared to act. This chapter will show you how to become a magnet for the opportunities and people that can change your life. Ready to make the shift? Let's dive in.

Owning the millionaire's room

Friends often ask me, "How is it that you walk into a room full of millionaires—many wealthier than you—and instantly become the centre of attention? How can you be so bold, yet have everyone eager to work with you again and again, regardless of origin, language, culture, or etiquette?"

The truth is, my power doesn't come from the numbers in my bank account—though I certainly appreciate a healthy balance. People see me the way I see myself: big, bold, and someone who gets things done. It's not an act or a façade. People sense that I'm genuinely a part of their story, woven into their lives and beliefs. This genuine connection fosters immediate trust and respect.

Let me share a little secret with you. People look at you, but they see your partner (the person in your mirror). Before any important meeting or event, I make sure that my partner is ready and happy, regardless of the current situation, stress, or fear. And people see it.

You see over 1000 people every day! Don't be boring.

Did you know that the average city dweller—someone who uses public transportation, works in a sizable company, and engages in typical social activities—might cross paths with 1,000 to 5,000 people daily? Think about that. How many of those people are truly noticeable?

To attract amazing people and great opportunities, you need to be **positively noticeable**. You need to make an impact on people's lives, make them feel great, and inspire them with your wisdom and the person you aspire to be. When you elevate others, you elevate yourself, becoming a magnet for the extraordinary.

Boring is meaningless

With each encounter, I strive to bring meaningful moments—whether it's putting a smile on someone's face, making them feel incredible, or igniting a positive change. Just as countless people have impacted me and shaped who I am today, I aim to be that spark for others.

Small People Never Attract Big Things

As we've touched on before, **small people never attract big things**. This isn't about stature or status; it's about mindset. If you see yourself as insignificant or unworthy, you'll unconsciously repel the very opportunities that could elevate your life. A limited mindset narrows your vision, causing you to miss possibilities right in front of you.

Think about it: Have you ever missed an opportunity because you didn't recognize its potential at the time? Maybe you declined an invitation, overlooked a new connection, or dismissed an idea because it didn't fit within your limited perception. These missed chances accumulate, keeping you anchored in the same place. The good news is that you're reading this book. By the end of this chapter, you'll have everything you need to **grow bigger** and own the room on any occasion.

Everybody Has Problems—So What?

Yes, I know. Let me tell you straight: **Everyone has problems**. It doesn't matter how much money you have or how many businesses you own. But the real issue arises when you let your current challenges define who you are. When you allow them to consume your attention and drain the energy you need to take off.

People don't want to hear about your problems every day—they have enough on their own plates. They want to be inspired by the person you can be—by your mission, your goals, and your dedication. When you let immediate necessities take over, you lose your position to small things. And in doing so, **you attract small things**.

Of course, you should share your challenges with friends and family and seek the help you might need. But when you embark on a journey of growth, you change your emotional state. You step forward as the person you aspire to be, not the one losing to ongoing issues. By embracing this mindset, you not only elevate yourself but also become a beacon for others, attracting amazing opportunities and inspiring those around you.

Do Things That Make You Happy

Because when you're smiling, the whole world smiles with you.

There's a beautiful song from 1928 that captures this sentiment perfectly:

"Oh, when you're smilin'
When you're smilin'
The whole world smiles with you..."

Take a moment to listen to this song by Louis Armstrong or Frank Sinatra. Let the joyful melody wash over you, feel the smile spread across your face, and let that warmth fill your heart before you continue reading.

You need to dedicate time each week to do the things that make you truly happy. It's astonishing how quickly life's demands can sap your energy and how many people might, knowingly or unknowingly, try to steer you away from your passions. But here's the truth: **when you do what you love, you radiate happiness**. And when you're happy, you're in the perfect emotional state to meet the right people and attract big opportunities. So go ahead—mark it in your calendar. Schedule time to indulge in what brings you joy.

For me, some of the things that make my heart sing are dancing tango and savouring exquisite wines. Wherever I travel, I search for local milongas (tango events) and explore the region's wines. In fact, I've met some of my closest friends and sealed some of my greatest deals while doing just that. People with shared passions come from all walks of life, and it's incredibly likely that you'll meet your next friend, business colleague, or life-changing opportunity while immersed in what you love.

By embracing what makes you happy, you not only enrich your own life but also become a magnet for others. Happiness is contagious, and when you're genuinely enjoying life, you attract amazing people and opportunities naturally. So ask yourself: **What makes your heart rumble with joy?** Whatever it is, make time for it. Your future self will thank you.

The $1,750,000 Napkin Deal Signed Over Côtes du Rhône

Let me share a personal story that illustrates the power of doing what you love.

When I had just started my financial business in the UK, we needed to cut a deal with the nation's biggest credit agency. At that time, we couldn't commit to the volumes they were asking for. We were just beginning our journey to redefine online credit in the UK. My team had contacted them multiple times, and I sensed they were growing annoyed with us. I asked my team to invite the regional sales manager to our office.

The meeting started cold and to the point. "With your size, this is the best price we can approve," he stated. I knew that in this emotional state, we wouldn't achieve the breakthrough we needed. So I shifted the conversation entirely. I shared my passion for tango and wine and how I built businesses around the world by doing what I love.

When you speak about things you love, you shine.

Positive energy radiates. At some point, the regional sales manager mentioned that his daughter dreamed of learning tango. We also discovered that he was a wine lover. Our conversation transformed. We weren't talking finance, credit checks, or artificial intelligence anymore. We talked about tango, travelling the world, and great wine experiences—the things we cared about most.

My employees left the room, and I remained with the regional manager from the credit agency. I stepped out and called a friend of mine, a famous tango teacher in the UK. We arranged an amazing dinner followed by a milonga and a first tango lesson for his daughter.

We went to the restaurant and had an unforgettable evening. We signed the contract—with better prices than anyone could have imagined—on a napkin at the restaurant, sealed with another bottle of Côtes du Rhône. After that, we went to the milonga. The day after, our secretaries talked to formalize the napkin contract and realized we'd made some errors in the calculations (perhaps we had one bottle too many). They dealt with the technicalities and we still got a deal we couldn't have even asked for.

His daughter continued with tango, met her future husband there, and we are all still very good friends.

Cultivating a World-Class Mindset

Becoming a magnet for opportunities requires adopting a world-class mindset. This means thinking bigger, aiming higher, and refusing to settle for mediocrity. Here's how to cultivate this mindset:

1. Expand Your Vision

To attract big opportunities, you need to see beyond your current circumstances. Believe that you are worthy of greatness and capable of achieving extraordinary things. When you elevate your self-image, you begin to notice opportunities that were previously invisible.

2. Surround Yourself with Greatness

Your environment shapes you. Surround yourself with people who inspire, challenge, and support your growth. Connect with mentors, join groups of high achievers, and immerse yourself in environments that elevate your thinking.

3. Take Massive Action

Opportunities favour the bold. Don't wait for things to happen—make them happen. Take initiative, be proactive, and pursue your goals relentlessly. Action creates momentum, and momentum attracts even more opportunities.

4. Cultivate Resilience

Big opportunities often come with big challenges. Develop the resilience to handle setbacks and persist in the face of adversity. Resilience ensures that you can sustain success once you achieve it.

5. Ask Powerful Questions

Instead of accepting things at face value, ask questions that dig deeper. "What if?" "Why not?" "How can this be improved?" Questions stimulate your mind to see possibilities others miss.

Closing Thoughts

Opportunities are everywhere, but only those who are prepared can seize them. Become a powerful magnet for opportunities, and watch as your life transforms in ways you never imagined. Being an opportunity magnet has a strong ripple effect, the waves expand beyond your direct actions.

Reflection notes

ACTIONS TO TAKE

-
-
-
-
-
-

IDEAS

-
-
-
-
-
-
-
-
-
-
-
-

ILLUSTRATION

Draw here the first visualization that comes to mind:

GRATITUDE

PERSONAL NOTES

Reflection notes

ACTIONS TO TAKE

IDEAS

ILLUSTRATION

Draw here the first visualization that comes to mind:

GRATITUDE

PERSONAL NOTES

CHAPTER 5

NOTHING HAS MEANING OTHER THAN THE MEANING YOU GIVE IT

High emotions create low intelligence positions. Use it to your advantage

Let's dive into a powerful idea: **Nothing has meaning other than the meaning you give it.**

Previously, we've discussed several key concepts:

1. High emotions create low intelligence positions.
2. The one with more energy wins.
3. Creating positional advantages as a habit.
4. Your thoughts create emotions, which impact your actions and alter your results.
5. Clarity is power.

Life, people, and events constantly provide stimuli that trigger our responses, emotions, and thoughts—often without our permission.

The "Angry hour"

When I moved from Buenos Aires to Berlin, I couldn't get used to the flood of brown envelopes filled with official letters arriving at my doorstep. Every week started with these intimidating letters. Each time I received one, I felt stressed and ineffective for the entire day. I was letting these letters hold power over my own position—**a big mistake**.

After a few years, I realized I couldn't change the system to serve my personal position, no matter how much I tried. So, I decided to assign a different meaning to these actions I couldn't control. Instead of starting my day with a sense of urgency to tackle problems others imposed on me, I developed a powerful morning routine to set my own stage. I didn't let anyone interfere. The first two hours of the day became mine to plan my game.

I also stopped picking up my letters daily. I collected them once a week and allocated a specific time to deal with them—just 90 minutes every Friday, which I called my **"angry time."** Remember the deflection strategy we discussed earlier? This was it in action. I moved the letters aside so I could advance on my journey, dedicating a focused and limited amount of time to handle other people's priorities. Yes, sometimes I had to pay a bit more on bills due to delays but believe me, gaining so much quality time to focus on my journey made those extra costs the best investment I could make.

1. Nothing Has Meaning Other Than the Meaning You Give It

High emotions create low intelligence positions, and as we've seen, emotions are energies that impact your actions. You don't want to make critical decisions that may have a ripple effect on your journey while you're in a low-intelligence state.

We live in a rapidly changing environment. Our context provides us with many reasons to get emotional daily. Sometimes, people we love do things that upset us. Other times, stress about bills or finances weighs us down. Mistakes we've made or goals we haven't achieved can haunt us. Every day, people and situations trigger our emotions.

But here's the thing: **You can't control these external events.** They will happen regardless. The only thing you can control is the meaning you assign to them and the level of emotional engagement you choose to have. Don't let others put you in a low-intelligence working state. It becomes a major obstacle, preventing you from seeing things clearly and adding more stress—a vicious cycle.

Passion and Emotional Sensitivity

When you do things you love, you become deeply attached to your product or offering. This puts you in a sensitive place. You'll notice things others might overlook and care deeply about aspects that others might find trivial. This heightened sensitivity can lead to frustration, and you may find yourself blaming others.

Recognize these signals and remind yourself that while following your passion is wonderful, you can't allow the consequent emotions to reduce your intelligence level and lead to poor decisions. Win your own passion position by first identifying when you're becoming overly emotional, and second, understanding how it affects you in the moment. You can't expect others to own your dream, but you can lead them to help you fulfil it.

On the other hand, you can use emotions to get the best out of yourself and others. I've helped people realize life-changing insights by challenging them with bold questions, disagreeing with their perspectives, and pushing them to think differently. While it might stir strong emotions initially, it often leads to profound breakthroughs.

The Brazil Trip: When Small Things Seem Big

One story I often share is about my trip to Brazil—a lifelong dream. I wanted to dance in the carnival, enjoy the beautiful beaches, and wake up sipping fresh coconut water. I worked hard for three years and finally saved enough money for this joyous adventure.

On the very first day, at the train station, someone stole my wallet containing money and important documents. This small incident triggered such powerful emotions that it shaped my entire journey. I wasn't happy; I was worried and angry, blaming everyone and everything around me. I just wanted to go back home. I didn't yet have the mental resilience to see beyond my passion and understand that sometimes, small setbacks are just that—small.

2. Accepting the Broken Vase

When a beautiful flower vase falls and shatters into pieces, you can pick up the fragments and glue them back together. It might hold flowers again and look almost the same, but it will never be the original vase.

In life, relationships, and various situations along our journey, things will fall apart. Trust and friendships built over years can break in a single moment of high emotion and low intelligence. The high energy required to piece things back together can swing your emotional state to unhealthy places, disrupting the balance you need to achieve your goals. And even if you manage to mend things, they may never be the same again.

As hard as it may be to accept, understanding this reality is crucial. You can't allow bad feelings to pile up inside you, creating another layer of chaos around the winner you are. It's all connected, and letting negativity fester can diminish your magnetism for opportunities.

People may remind you of past mistakes and try to make you pay for them repeatedly. I dedicate a full section to this topic because many people have emotional strings that make it harder for them to move forward. Realizing that something is broken and allowing yourself to move on is a powerful healing process. Accept it and move forward, or eliminate it from your life. But don't let it drain your energy.

At the same time, when you're responsible for breaking the vase—or even when others think you are—you should ask for forgiveness. Say you're sorry and mean it from your heart. In the heat of the moment, it's extremely hard because you're hurt, and your emotional state is off balance. Notice how much energy and focus it consumes.

But here's the powerful secret: **When you apologize and seek forgiveness, you do it for yourself.** It's about releasing yourself from negative energy and stress. You pass the burden to someone else. Whether they forgive you or not is their decision, but you'll feel as if a heavy weight has been lifted from your shoulders.

Closing Thoughts

Remember, nothing has meaning other than the meaning you give it. By controlling the interpretations you assign to events and managing your emotional responses, you maintain clarity and power over your actions. This mental resilience allows you to stay on your critical path, make better decisions, and keep moving forward on your journey to prosper by doing what you love.

By embracing these insights, you equip yourself to navigate life's challenges with greater wisdom and strength. Keep moving forward, and remember that you have the power to define your own reality.

Reflection notes

ACTIONS TO TAKE

-
-
-
-
-
-

IDEAS

-
-
-
-
-
-
-
-
-
-
-
-

ILLUSTRATION

Draw here the first visualization that comes to mind:

GRATITUDE

PERSONAL NOTES

Reflection notes

ACTIONS TO TAKE

-
-
-
-
-
-

IDEAS

-
-
-
-
-
-
-
-
-
-
-
-

ILLUSTRATION

Draw here the first visualization that comes to mind:

GRATITUDE

PERSONAL NOTES

CHAPTER 6

MIND THE GAP AND UNIVERSAL EFFECTS

The ripple effect, synchronicity and eliminating open loops

Everything suggests something—it can support or disrupt your journey.

We didn't create the universe, and we surely don't manage it. But understanding some of its rules and effects can help you cross many bridges most won't even see. The powerful ideas and universal effects explained in this chapter can help you step along your invisible bridge with energy and focus. You can also use them to become stronger and increase the clarity of your path. I'll keep it practical so you can use it instantly. Please pay extra attention to the feelings and ideas that come to mind as you read this chapter. **Read it and mean it!** Bring it into your world; it will help you grow.

Open Loops Are the Home for Confusion

Our brains don't like open loops. When you look at a picture of a circle with a small gap, your mind immediately focuses on that point. In life, we need to close open loops to keep our focus on our critical path and gain positional advantages daily. Open loops drain our energy and dissolve our focus.

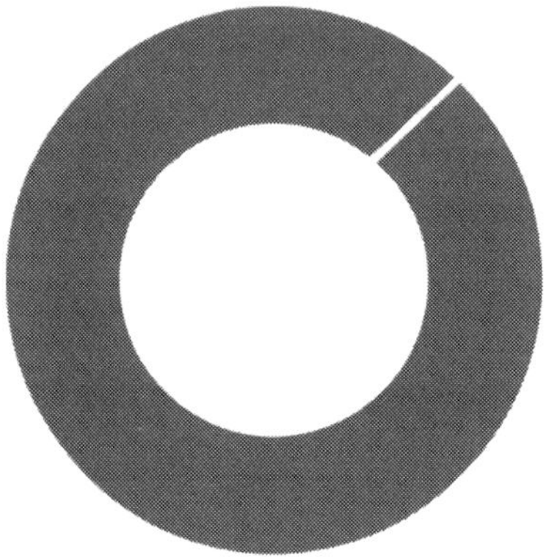

Open loops could be little things you don't like doing but are there, or bigger things you always delay. They can be in relationships, with friends, challenges, tasks you need to complete, and many other areas. The most important thing is to **recognize the open loops and deal with them—or accept them!**

Most people, including me, tend to keep open loops for a long time because they're not ready to deal with the consequences. But as we've discussed before, open loops are the background noise on your critical path. They're dangerously powerful and will not let you become as big and amazing as you want to be. If you decide to accept those open loops, do it fully.

For those of us who are married, I'm sure you can come up with a short, 100-page list of open loops that take your energy and focus. Jokes aside, let's try the following exercise.

Exercise: Eliminating Open Loops

Be honest with yourself and make a list of all the open loops you have—things that aren't clicking well in your relationships and business, Things that annoy you, making you angry, changing your emotional state. Things you defer again and again. Write them down and note your steps to eliminate or how you fully accept them.

Synchronicity

Have you ever had the feeling that someone is looking at you from behind?

Let me share a story about synchronicity that changed my life in many beautiful ways.

It was a freezing night just a couple of weeks before Christmas. The small airplane finally landed in Steamboat Springs, Colorado. I went there to meet potential investors for my Wall Street-based cybersecurity company. I realized quite quickly that my expensive double-breasted suit, elegant pocket square, and Italian leather shoes were probably not the most suitable attire. But well, it was too late to change.

Everything was white with snow. I arrived at the hotel late at night and couldn't sleep. I had to prepare my presentation for old-money people living on the mountain. My brain started to wander—what am I doing here?

Around 4 a.m., I decided to try and find the hotel kitchen to see if I could get myself a coffee and start preparing for the 9 a.m. meeting. It was so dark, and I was trying to find out how to turn on the lights in the small dining room. As I searched for the switch, I felt something go right through me. I felt that there was someone else in the room, looking right at me. I froze, and my brain started to imagine the scariest scenarios. I didn't dare turn around and started to think about how to do it. Should I jump over the table and go to the floor? Should I turn around slowly to not scare anyone? The feeling was so strong and eerie.

In the end, I decided to turn around slowly, and I saw, on the other side of the room, a man sitting, dressed in black, reading a book with a flashlight. He didn't even take his eyes off the book to look at me. As my senses started to recover from this strange experience, I decided to get a bit closer to him to see if he was real or just my imagination. From afar, I noticed that the book he was reading was the Bible. I approached a bit closer. Out of nowhere, he asked me, "Are you the Wall Street boy who came to town for a meeting?"

I was so shocked. I mumbled, "Yes, I am."

And that's how I met my lifelong friend and mentor, Pastor Dr. Johnny Cortez. We spoke about life, people, and everything until 8 a.m. I hadn't prepared my presentation and already knew the meeting with the investors wasn't going to work. I wasn't ready! I didn't have proper clothes or shoes to wear; they were going to hate me! No chance I would ever come back with money from that little town. I thanked Johnny for the inspiring conversation and went off to the meeting.

I arrived at their farm for the meeting. People wore boots and country attire, and there I was in my Italian suit. I took out my laptop and started to prepare, waiting for the father of the family to arrive. I figured it would be a waste of time asking for a projector. He came in and said, "Let's go eat. We'll do the meeting at the diner." I don't have to explain how awkward it was. We went to the diner and started talking about life values and other things. As a Wall Street-trained entrepreneur, I was ready to cut to the chase and talk about money...

And then, Johnny walked in.

Yes, the same Johnny I had met just a few hours ago, still holding the Bible in his hand. Everybody gave him respect and welcomed him to the table. He told them about our encounter and that I was very stressed about the presentation and everything we had talked about. We had a wonderful three-hour breakfast. We spoke very briefly about my cybercrime prevention product.

As we finished breakfast, I was a bit confused. "When should I do my presentation?" I asked. Their answer was, "We don't need it. Just give us the account details so we can wire the money."

I remained good friends with Johnny to this day. We've had many more defining moments together.

The Power of Synchronicity

Synchronicity is an intriguing concept that suggests seemingly random events or experiences are connected in an unseen but natural way. First proposed by Carl Jung in the 1920s, it is based on the idea that everything in the universe is interconnected and that certain events may have deeper meanings. Recognizing these meaningful coincidences can lead to personal growth and success by better understanding our environment.

I'm sure you've encountered this phenomenon in your life before. Here are some everyday examples of synchronicity:

- **Thinking about someone you haven't seen in years, and then, out of the blue, they call or send you a message.** It might indicate that reconnecting with your old friend is important for your growth and development.
- **You're thinking about buying a new car model, and suddenly you start seeing this car everywhere.** Or a specific colour, or a designer bag. Don't overthink it; you know it happens—you've experienced it. So why don't you direct your brain and thoughts toward the things you want to achieve? Let it be aware that this is what you want amid the information and background noise. It will help you focus.
- **Have you ever been in a conversation with a stranger and suddenly finished their sentence for them?** It may indicate that you are on the same wavelength as that person.

Mind the existence of synchronicity occasions in your life. Note them and try to understand what they suggest and if they can help your journey. You may be surprised.

The Ripple Effect

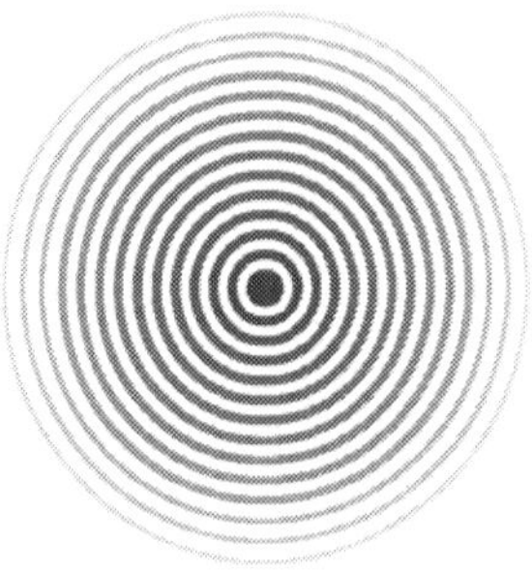

The ripple effect refers to how a single action or event can cause a series of consequences that spread outward, much like ripples expanding across water when a stone is dropped into it. The term "ripple effect" is rooted in observations from physics and nature. The concept is established in fields like sociology, economics, psychology, and personal development to describe how actions can lead to a chain of reactions.

This is one of my favourite ideas. In fact, crossing the invisible bridge in any given position is key to initiating many ripple effects that will help you prosper by doing what you love, leveraging the impact of indirect consequences. Let me give you a practical example I've followed for years:

Adopting a Daily Habit That Enhances Productivity and Well-Being

You start practising mindfulness meditation for 10 minutes each morning.

- **Immediate Impact:** You feel calmer and more focused at the start of your day.
- **Short-Term Effects:** Enhanced focus leads to better decision-making and efficiency at work. You achieve more in less time.
- **Long-Term Outcomes:** Consistent productivity gains result in career advancement or successful business growth. Improved well-being strengthens personal relationships and overall life satisfaction. You attract more effective people and expand your network, opening the horizon to many opportunities.

A simple change in your daily routine creates ripples that enhance various facets of your life, demonstrating the power of small actions in improving your position.

By embracing small, purposeful habits, you harness the power of the ripple effect. Each intentional act becomes a stepping stone, leading you toward greater prosperity and fulfilment. It's a testament to how understanding your position and making moves with clarity—no matter how small—can set in motion a wave of positive change that carries you, and those around you, closer to success.

Closing Thoughts

Understanding and leveraging universal effects like open loops, synchronicity, and the ripple effect can profoundly impact your journey. By closing open loops, you free up mental energy to focus on your critical path. By recognizing synchronicity, you become more attuned to meaningful coincidences that can guide you. By initiating positive ripple effects through small actions, you can create significant, lasting change in your life.

Remember, everything suggests something—it can support or disrupt your journey. Choose to interpret and act on these signals in ways that propel you forward. Mind the gap, embrace the universal effects, and continue stepping across your invisible bridges with energy and focus.

Reflection notes

ACTIONS TO TAKE

-
-
-
-
-
-

IDEAS

-
-
-
-
-
-
-
-
-
-
-
-

ILLUSTRATION

Draw here the first visualization that comes to mind:

GRATITUDE

PERSONAL NOTES

Reflection notes

ACTIONS TO TAKE

IDEAS

ILLUSTRATION

Draw here the first visualization that comes to mind:

GRATITUDE

PERSONAL NOTES

CHAPTER 7

GETTING THROUGH THE TIPPING POINT

Change Releases Energy—Don't Give In to Quick Fixes

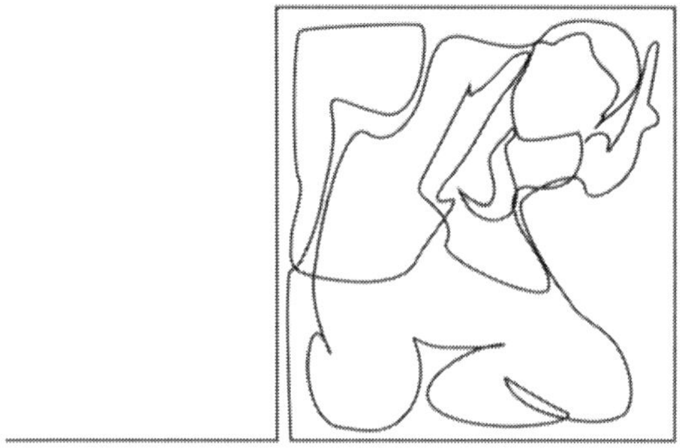

Congratulations! You have reached the final chapter of Part One of this book. By now, I hope you have gained greater clarity, understanding, and motivation on your path to prosperity. This chapter imparts the last bit of wisdom and tools you will need to stay on the journey and resist the tempting quit offers from your own mind. In the next section, we'll apply everything we've discussed with hands-on practical tools and templates that will save you time and money.

We All Live in a Box

We all live in a box. Sometimes, what we desire lies outside of that box, and as we've seen before, the things we want so much can blind us to the steps required by our current position—the "invisible bridges." The reward for a job well done is a bigger box. A bigger box creates different ripples and attracts people and opportunities that are larger in scale.

Along the way, we must remember that other people don't always want what we want. You need to lead them to invest their energy in getting you to where you want to be.

Most people never grow out of their box because they are afraid of failure or judgment. Even those who try often fail. We've already explained how positional thinking strategies help you find the next best step. But the focus of this chapter is on the tipping point and the stress created every time you need to cross the bridge from where you are to a better position.

The Environment Is Stronger Than Your Will

The process of change and transformation releases a lot of energy and creates stress—stress from fear, lack of clarity, environmental factors, and background noise. You need to minimize the amount of toxins and open loops in your environment as you go through this process.

Change is not always something you choose. In many cases, it's something you must do as a result of energy from the environment—your context. Whether you choose to do it or are forced into it, the level of stress is often unpleasant.

We have been given an oversized brain that always tries to keep us safe and balanced. As we face stress, the brain offers us magical painkillers or the constant option to quit. The alternative names for these "magical painkillers" are addictions—addictions to alcohol, drugs, excessive shopping, unhealthy relationships, or endless scrolling on mobile phones.

Addictions may temporarily reduce the pain you feel as a result of stress, but they will not remove the stress. Over time, you may need them more and more to deal with even lower levels of stress. It's a vicious cycle you need to avoid.

Earlier, I mentioned that the reward for a job well done is a bigger job. As long as you have passion within you, the process of growing is never-ending. There will always be emotions, stress, unknown elements, successes, and failures. But the rewards are absolutely amazing—they are life-changing. And because you are reading this book, you have already decided not to be confined to a box that's too small to let you be the amazing person you truly are.

Three tools that I constantly use to manage stress and help me stay focused during life's transformations are the **Code of Honor (COH)**, **Non-Sleep Deep Rest (NSDR)** protocols and **Internal Motivation Protocol**. As you follow your path, you'll find the tools that work for you and integrate them into your daily routine.

Your Personal Code of Honor

In the absence of rules, people create rules that don't serve your journey.

I used to be a quitter. When challenges arose, I often looked for shiny opportunities elsewhere, and my mind was eager to provide them—just to make me abandon the journey. It took me many years with top coaches, numerous failures, and significant resources to master the art of crossing invisible bridges and dealing with the consequent stress. I'm sharing these insights with you so you can take them and apply them today.

Stop losing the battle to your own mind. Think about it: How many times have you told yourself, "I need to go to the gym," "I should reduce sugar consumption," or "I want to learn a new language"?

Inside you, there is a winner, covered with layers of life-given sediments and scars—limiting beliefs, stress, and emotional wounds from past experiences. These layers prevent you from seeing your position clearly and make every desirable change in life seem much harder than it really is. When things seem harder, most people don't even try, and many who do try give in to their mind's suggestions to quit or seek quick fixes. But not you.

Crafting Your Personal Code of Honor

Facing a challenging journey requires more than just determination—it calls for a solid foundation that keeps you grounded and focused. A personal code of honour serves as this foundation, acting as a compass that guides your decisions and actions. It's a conscious commitment to uphold certain values, rules, and agreements that reflect your true self and highest aspirations.

- **Values** are the core principles that define who you are and what you stand for. They might include integrity, courage, compassion, perseverance, or honesty. Begin by reflecting on what matters most to you. Ask yourself which qualities you admire in others and wish to embody. These values become the pillars of your code of honour, influencing every choice you make.

- **Rules** are the standards of behaviour you set for yourself based on your values. They are actionable commitments that direct how you conduct yourself, especially when faced with obstacles. For example, if you value integrity, a rule might be, "I will always speak the truth, even when it's difficult." If you value perseverance, a rule could be, "I will not give up in the face of adversity."

- **Agreements** are promises you make to yourself and, if you choose, to others. They solidify your commitment to your values and rules, serving as a personal contract that holds you accountable. Agreements might include statements like, "I agree to treat myself with kindness and patience," or "I agree to continuously seek growth and learning." By articulating these agreements, you create a sense of responsibility that motivates you to stay true to your path.

By thoughtfully defining your values, establishing clear rules, and making sincere agreements, you craft a personal code of honour that empowers you to navigate your journey with confidence and integrity. This code becomes a touchstone—

a source of strength and guidance—that helps you remain aligned with your authentic self, no matter what challenges arise.

Non-Sleep Deep Rest (NSDR) – A 10-Minute Practice

I personally use NSDR at least once a day as part of my daily routine, which I will share with you later in the book.

Non-Sleep Deep Rest (NSDR) is a practice that allows you to relax quickly and deeply, tapping into your body's natural ability to restore and rejuvenate without requiring actual sleep. Research has shown that NSDR offers numerous health benefits on both mental and physical levels. It's fantastic for enhancing learning and memory, reducing stress, and boosting cognitive capacity. The beauty of NSDR lies in its flexibility—it can be practised at any time of day or night, fitting seamlessly into your daily routine.

NSDR works by guiding you into a state of deep relaxation through specific breathing techniques and focused attention. By slowing down your heart rate and calming your nervous system, you gain control over your state of mind. This practice helps shift your brain from a state of thinking, stress, planning, or anticipation—whether positive or negative—to one of pure sensation and tranquillity.

Own your source of motivation

Your motivation must not be exclusively derived from others' feedback. *When you put your motivation in the hands of others, your critical path may look like one step forward, two steps back.*

It's vital to understand that the most meaningful motivation comes from within. While external rewards like praise or recognition can feel gratifying, they often make your drive dependent on factors beyond your control. By cultivating an internal reward system, you take charge of your own motivation. When you acknowledge and celebrate your efforts and progress, you reinforce your commitment and fuel your momentum.

Start by recognizing each small victory along the way. Whether it's completing a task, overcoming a challenge, or making incremental progress toward your goal, take a moment to appreciate your hard work. This self-acknowledgement boosts your energy and focus, helping you push through obstacles with greater ease. Remember, by rewarding yourself internally, you build a sustainable source of motivation that propels you forward, regardless of external circumstances. You keep control of your position and progress.

Build Your Own Protocols

Every successful person has morning, evening, and daily protocols. Protocols help to keep you in the game—healthy, energized, and focused. They help you deal with stress and increase your mental, physical, and cognitive capacity. In essence, they help you become a much better, stronger, and bigger version of yourself. And we already know that big people attract big opportunities and like-minded individuals.

> Join our community (Chapter 15) to get exclusive invitations to the upcoming **Protocols Master-Class Training** events.

Closing Thoughts

Change releases energy and propels you forward, but it also brings challenges. By understanding the dynamics of transformation and equipping yourself with tools like a personal code of honour and practices like NSDR, you position yourself to navigate the tipping points in your journey successfully.

Remember, the most significant distance to cross is often within your own mind. Embrace the journey, harness your internal motivation, and build the protocols that will support your growth. You've come this far—now is the time to push forward and realize the incredible potential that lies ahead.

Let's move on to the next part of the book, where we'll put these principles into action with practical tools and strategies designed to help you prosper by doing what you love.

Reflection notes

ACTIONS TO TAKE

IDEAS

ILLUSTRATION

Draw here the first visualization that comes to mind:

GRATITUDE

PERSONAL NOTES

Reflection notes

ACTIONS TO TAKE

IDEAS

ILLUSTRATION

Draw here the first visualization that comes to mind:

GRATITUDE

PERSONAL NOTES

PART 2

Practical Tools, Templates and Cheat-Sheets

CHAPTER 8

WHY YOU LOSE THE GAME OF WEALTH AND HOW TO FIX IT

Understand Your Current Position and Win It

Yes, we're going to talk money! But worry not—I'm going to keep it simple and focus on what truly makes a difference. In this chapter, we'll explore why you might be losing the game of wealth every day and what you can do to change it. It all comes down to understanding **three simple ideas**. When I share these concepts in my lectures, I often see jaws drop as people realize their position and immediately begin seeking solutions. When this happens to you, give yourself a pat on the shoulder—the change has begun. Don't let your hard-earned money lose value; take steps to strengthen your position and secure your future. Let's start.

Point 1: The Wrong Trade—You're Wasting Your Most Precious Asset

Consider this business scenario: If I sell you a building for $1 million today, but tomorrow I can't buy it back for the same price because its value has increased significantly, did I make a good deal? Obviously not. There are better ways to leverage assets.

Now, ask yourself: What is the asset most people trade daily to make money and live the life they want?

That asset is your **time**—your most precious and non-renewable resource.

Whether you earn $10 per hour or $1,000 per hour, the fact remains: **You cannot buy back that hour tomorrow for the same price—or any price at all**. Once time is spent, it's gone forever. Trading your finite hours for money is a losing proposition in the long run.

As you progress through life, you have fewer and fewer hours left. Why continue exchanging this diminishing asset for money? It's crucial to internalize this concept. You don't have to overhaul your life overnight but consider starting small. What if you could allocate just 10% of your time differently? What if you aimed to work fewer hours but make 50% more money?

To achieve this, you need to find the right financial vehicles and strategies that allow your money to work for you, rather than you working for money. But you can't find these solutions until you shift your mindset and recognize that **trading time for money isn't the path to wealth**.

Every time you sell an hour of your life for a set amount of money, you're making a trade you can't reverse. Your time is your most valuable asset—stop wasting it by trading it away.

By understanding and embracing this concept, you can begin to seek out opportunities that maximize your time and income. Invest in assets that grow in value, develop passive income streams, and focus on strategies that don't require you to exchange time for money directly. Your journey to wealth starts with recognizing the true value of your time and making deliberate choices to protect and enhance it within your own risk/reward appetite.

Point 2: The Impact of Currency Devaluation

The second crucial point to understand is **currency devaluation**—a silent force that erodes your wealth over time. Often experienced as rising costs of living, inflation, or economic recessions, currency devaluation makes life increasingly expensive and is largely beyond individual control.

Consider this: Over the past several decades, the purchasing power of the U.S. dollar has significantly declined due to inflation. For example, what you could buy for **$10,000 in 1970 would cost you over $75,000 today**. This means that the dollar has lost a substantial portion of its value over the last 50 years.

But why does this happen? Governments, in an effort to manage economic policies and address national debt, often increase the money supply by printing more money. While this can stimulate the economy in the short term, it leads to inflation—**more money chasing the same amount of goods and services**—which reduces the value of each individual dollar.

Your Slice of the Pie Gets Smaller

This is especially painful for people like me who love a big piece of apple pie, served with vanilla ice cream and coffee. Okay, back to money.

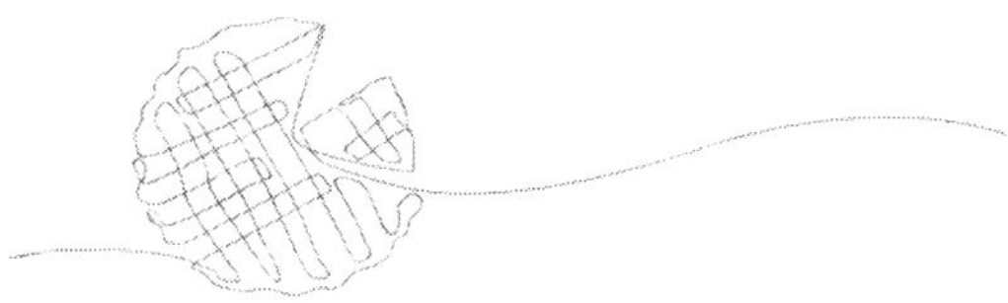

Imagine your money as a share in the global economy. When more money is printed without a corresponding increase in actual value (like goods or services), the value of each "share" decreases. **Your slice of the economic pie gets smaller**, and your money buys less than it did before. Meanwhile, those with significant wealth often have access to sophisticated financial instruments and assets that can protect them from currency devaluation—such as real estate, stocks, or commodities like gold. But most people don't have these protections, leaving their savings vulnerable to the eroding effects of inflation.

Things Will Not Get Any Easier

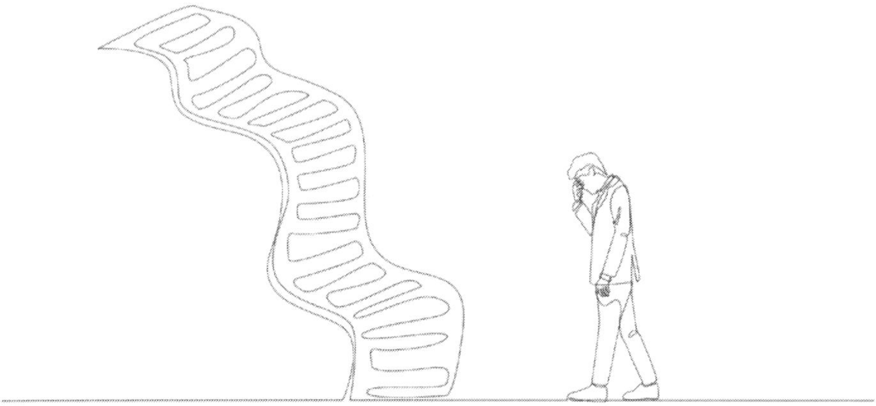

Waiting for things to get better isn't a viable strategy. The devaluation of currency is an ongoing process, and without proactive steps, your financial position will continue to weaken over time. **Money sitting idle in the bank loses value every day**, buying less tomorrow than it does today.

It's essential to recognize this reality and take control of your financial future. By understanding how currency devaluation affects your wealth, you can make informed decisions to protect and grow your assets, rather than watching them diminish.

Together with the first point about trading your time for money, this highlights why you might be losing the wealth game every single day. **Your position weakens as you move forward unless you take deliberate action** to change the way you manage your assets and income.

Key Takeaways:

- Currency devaluation wears down your purchasing power over time.
- Inflation reduces the value of money, making everything more expensive.

- Relying solely on traditional savings means losing wealth due to inflation.
- Wealthy individuals often use assets and investments to hedge against inflation.
- You must proactively seek ways to protect and grow your wealth to avoid falling behind.

By acknowledging these economic realities, you empower yourself to seek strategies that safeguard your financial well-being within your level of risk/reward appetite.

Point 3: Health, Wealth, Love, and Happiness—The Universal Desires

There are over 200,000 words in the English language, yet when we send greetings to the people we love, we often use the same four words: **health, wealth, love, and happiness**. Regardless of culture, language, status, or the amount of money in our bank accounts, these wishes resonate universally. It's fascinating how different we think we are, yet we all desire the same fundamental things for ourselves and our loved ones.

Now, let's take a moment to reflect on these four pillars in relation to your current position:

- **Health**: Is your health improving with time, or is it deteriorating as you age, becoming more expensive and challenging to maintain?
- **Wealth**: Is the money you have gaining value, or is it losing purchasing power every single day due to inflation and economic shifts?
- **Happiness**: As challenges and stress accumulate, are you experiencing more joyful moments, or are they becoming fewer and farther between?
- **Love**: Are you engaged in work and activities that you love? Is it easier for you to accept differences as you get older? Are you more open to change with time?

Consider this: **Is your current position strengthening over time, or is it weakening?** By now, you likely know the answer.

On a Positive Note

I'm not trying to upset you—my mission is to help you prosper by doing things you love. But it's essential to recognize that if you don't take proactive steps, your wealth and overall position may continue to decline. Remember what we discussed earlier in this book: **taking control of your position is crucial.**

You can't control the context—in this case, the global financial system and the fact that we all, yes, you too, are getting older with time. But there are powerful things you can do to stay ahead of the curve:

1. Stay Healthy

Take care of your health; stay up to date with scientific advancements. There are amazing discoveries in longevity research that can change your life—they changed mine some years ago. I'll share some protocols from top scientific findings on the book's portal.

2. Make Your Money Work Harder

Ensure that your money earns at least **4% more than the average inflation level.** So if, for example, inflation is 3.5%, your money should make at least 7.5% per year, adjusted to your desired level of security.

> Get exclusive access to the financial vehicle I use to make 17%-135% on my money (Chapter 15)

3. Reclaim Your Time

Take at least **20% of the lost trade** (hours you work for other people) and find a financial vehicle that can get you at least **three times more** for these hours without you working.

In the next chapter, **"Finding Your $1,000,000 Product,"** we'll explore powerful tools to help you thrive despite a weakening position. By considering the above and utilizing your motivation, mission, passion, and energy, you'll transform your journey from a mere option into an absolute necessity.

Closing Thoughts

Understanding these fundamental concepts is the first step toward reclaiming control over your financial future. Recognize the true value of your time, be aware of how currency devaluation affects your wealth, and reflect on the universal desires of health, wealth, love, and happiness in your life.

Your journey to wealth and fulfilment starts now. It's time to take deliberate action, make informed decisions, and position yourself for success. Remember, you're not alone on this path—we're in this together, and I'm here to guide you every step of the way.

Let's move forward and discover how you can find your $1,000,000 product and unlock the prosperity you deserve.

Reflection notes

ACTIONS TO TAKE

-
-
-
-
-
-

IDEAS

-
-
-
-
-
-
-
-
-
-
-
-

ILLUSTRATION

Draw here the first visualization that comes to mind:

GRATITUDE

PERSONAL NOTES

Reflection notes

ACTIONS TO TAKE

-
-
-
-
-
-

IDEAS

-
-
-
-
-
-
-
-
-
-
-
-

ILLUSTRATION

Draw here the first visualization that comes to mind:

GRATITUDE

PERSONAL NOTES

CHAPTER 9

DISCOVER YOUR $1,000,000 PRODUCT

Find the Product That Suits You and Make a Fortune

Please fasten your seatbelts—we are heading toward the wealth take-off lane. We're about to explore a market-proven system that allows you to find the right product or service for you—a product that will make your passion shine and help you make a fortune doing what you love. But before we begin, let's review some critical elements you'll need along the way.

The $1,000,000 Product Formula

I earned my bachelor's and master's degrees at top universities, learning complicated strategies and financial models. But I developed my business and products using the simple formula we're about to discuss. You need to be honest with yourself and avoid trying to beautify your answers. This is meant to help you do the things that truly match you!

A great product or service is a combination of three main elements:

1. **Inner-Based Elements**
2. **Outer-Based Elements**
3. **Your Game Plan**

I've included a link that will give you access to my Mastermind coaching templates. You can get your product or service ready using millionaire-proven templates. In the last chapter of the book, you'll find the links and the codes you need.

The Inner-Based Elements

For years, I struggled with a major business problem that overshadowed all the fun of creating something amazing. Every time I started a new initiative, I thought I was doing things differently. I believed I had learned my lesson, yet the same problem kept happening. Until one of my coaches asked me to follow the model I'm teaching again.

At first, it sounded a bit odd, and the little voice in my head started shouting, "I already know it!" But I did it—just the way I want you to do it—and it solved my problem in such a powerful way. You may wonder what the problem was. Well, I had a pattern of losing everything once my ideas surpassed the one-million-dollar mark. I was an expert at taking initiatives from zero to the first million, but somehow, I always managed to lose everything afterwards. I crossed that bridge from zero to over a million so many times.

What made the difference for me this time was the way I approached it, and this should be your lesson learned from my personal experience:

- **Be Brutally Honest with Your Answers**

  It helped me understand that, in many cases, products that became more mature and solid were not aligned with my true passion. I simply started to slack on my own rules. Once you do that, it's only a matter of time until the momentum changes to a downhill direction.

- **Ignore the "I Know It" Mentality**

  These three words—"I know it"—are the most dangerous words for growth. Next time your brain tells you, "I know it" when trying to learn something new, politely say, "Thank you," and keep learning.

- **Stay True to Your Passion, Values, Mission, and Purpose**

  Stop doing things that go against your core beliefs and interests. Take this advice to heart and do it right from the first time.

The Inner Element Discovery Protocol

Grab a notebook and a pen (not your computer or phone). Go to a place where you love to read or work—perhaps a nice café or, in my case, a wine bar. Give yourself 20 minutes to answer the following questions. Be truthful with yourself; you don't have to impress anyone. It's all about you:

1. **When was the last time you did something that made your heart rumble?** What made you happy, feeling great, like you were on top of the world? What are the things that make you truly happy, and why? What feelings do those things trigger in you?

2. **What are your personal interests?** What do you love to do?

3. **What are your unique abilities and natural talents?** What do you do best?

4. **What is your purpose?** How can you help other people? When people ask for your advice, why do they come to you? What do they ask you about?

5. **What are you knowledgeable about?** What skills and knowledge have you acquired? These are your acquired skills, not your natural talents as in question 3.

6. **Why do you want to achieve your purpose?** Is it for money, peace of mind, becoming a better person, influencing others, being a hero, improving health, or for your ego? The journey to prosperity is a long one; you need to be very clear about why you're doing it.

7. **What major challenges have you overcome in your life, and do you think your personal lessons learned can help other people?** If you had to teach any topic from your personal life, what topics resonate with you?

The Outer-Based Elements

Let me start straight with the most important lesson of this chapter.

The outer elements are about your **target audience** and ensuring you provide the right product to high-demand sectors. The market is very clear about the high-demand topics. The biggest are:

- Health
- Wealth
- Success
- Beauty
- Relationships
- Sex
- Spirituality
- Personal Growth
- Technology

The secret to creating a powerful offering is to match your personal inner elements with these high-demand sectors and provide irresistible value based on what you discover about yourself.

The Outer-Based Protocol

1. The Target Market

Who are you going to serve? Who will pay to get the value you offer? Don't overthink this; just make a list right off the top of your head.

2. The Match Made in Heaven

Consider your honest answers to the inner elements protocol. How can you combine your topic with the high-demand topics mentioned above? Write down what you will offer to people interested in a specific high-demand topic.

3. Segmentation

Can you narrow it down to more specific groups you can serve? For example, people in a specific location, those with particular interests (like yoga enthusiasts), married people with kids over 40, or business professionals.

4. Value Proposition

For each of the groups you're going to serve, write one line about how you can serve them. What value does your product or service give them, and how does it help enhance their lives? Keep it short and simple. Example: "I help bakers double their income while working half the time."

5. The Approach

Think about how you can reach the groups and people who can benefit the most from the value you provide. Remember, you don't need to become a marketing expert, but you need to own your game and find the right people to do it for you.

Your Game Plan

Here's the brutally honest fact: If you want to prosper by doing what you love, you need to find the product or service that matches your inner elements and brings irresistible value to the right people—people who will appreciate and pay for the value you provide.

If Your inner and outer elements are not in tune, you'll burn your energy, money, and time trying to do things that aren't right for you.

At the beginning of this chapter, I shared some thinking methods of successful people. At this stage, your "little voice" might start saying things like, "Oh, but I'm not a marketing expert," or "I don't have the money for an expensive campaign," or "I don't know how to..."

Don't listen to that voice. Remember that no one knows everything. We're shifting now from **HOW** to do things to **WHO** can do it for us. In reality, if you match your inner elements correctly, the amount of money you'll need is much smaller because you'll be doing things that make you happy, make you shine, and make you appear amazing—and people will pay for that!

In the next chapter, we'll discover how to write your offer in a persuasive way that leaves no one indifferent.

It's also important to ensure that your product can get you the results you want. If not, you may need to develop more products or change your cost model. **Everything must be in harmony for the big money to follow.**

Key Takeaways

- **Align Inner and Outer Elements:** Your product or service should match your passions, talents, and purpose (inner elements) with market demand (outer elements).
- **Be Honest with Yourself:** Genuine self-reflection is crucial. Avoid the "I know it" mentality, and stay open to learning.
- **Identify Your Target Audience:** Clearly define who you will serve and how your offering provides value to them.
- **Craft a Clear Value Proposition:** Communicate succinctly how you help your audience and enhance their lives.
- **Focus on Your Strengths:** Do what makes you happy and allows you to shine; this attracts customers and opportunities.
- **Shift from How to Who:** You don't need to do everything yourself. Find the right people to help execute areas outside your expertise.

Closing Thoughts

Finding your $1,000,000 product is not about reinventing the wheel; it's about discovering what resonates deeply with you and aligns with what the market desires. By thoughtfully examining your inner passions and matching them with high-demand areas, you position yourself for success.

Remember, prosperity comes from doing what you love and delivering immense value to those who need it. Stay true to yourself, embrace the journey, and prepare to make a fortune doing what you love.

In the next chapter, we'll delve into crafting irresistible offers that captivate your audience and drive success. Let's continue this exciting journey together!

Reflection notes

ACTIONS TO TAKE

-
-
-
-
-
-

IDEAS

-
-
-
-
-
-
-
-
-
-
-
-

ILLUSTRATION

Draw here the first visualization that comes to mind:

GRATITUDE

PERSONAL NOTES

Reflection notes

ACTIONS TO TAKE

-
-
-
-
-
-

IDEAS

-
-
-
-
-
-
-
-
-
-
-
-

ILLUSTRATION

Draw here the first visualization that comes to mind:

GRATITUDE

PERSONAL NOTES

CHAPTER 10

A COFFEE WITH PASTOR JOHNNY C. AT A BOOKSHOP

Master the art of practical copywriting

Let me share with you a lesson in copywriting that I'll never forget—taught to me by my dear friend, Pastor Johnny C.

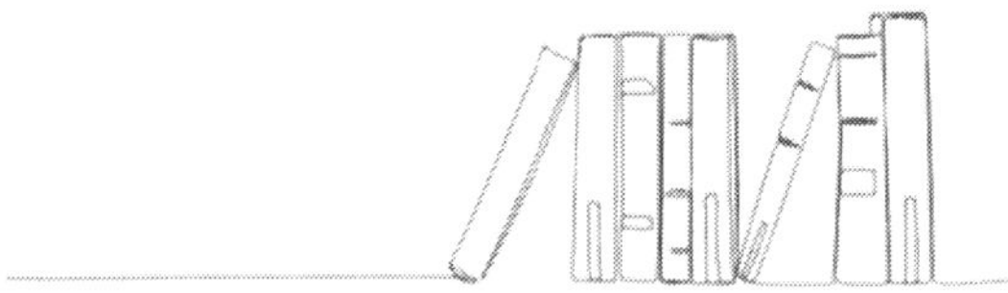

You might recall Johnny from my earlier story about the investors in Steamboat, Colorado. Fast forward many years, and he's now over 90, and we're still the best of friends. He moved to Houston, Texas, and whenever we meet, we talk for hours, sometimes even days. Johnny is bravely fighting terminal cancer, and I treasure every opportunity we have to share moments and life experiences.

Every time we get together, we visit a Barnes & Noble bookshop for coffee. We both love bookshops. Over the years, we've developed a little game that always leaves a lasting impression on us. Here's how it goes:

1. Choose Your Book Genre

We start by selecting a book genre—for example, personal development.

2. Find the Section

We head to that section in the store.

3. Scan the Shelves

Walking slowly, we scan the bookshelves without stopping.

4. Pick the Books That Catch Your Eye

We pick up the books that grab our attention as we go.

5. Discuss Our Selections

We return to the coffee table with our selections.

The idea is simple: with millions of books competing for space on the shelves, only the most captivating ones earn their spot, and those that don't sell eventually lose it. By scanning the book covers and picking those that grab our attention, we're practicing master-level copywriting.

Then, we go through each book and discuss why it caught our eye. What emotion did it trigger? Among all the bestsellers in the genre, what made this particular book stand out? We learn and take notes.

The lesson here is profound: **the way a book captures your attention can teach you how to craft headlines and subtitles that resonate.** Next time you write a headline or a subtitle, remember this exercise. Use what you've learned to trigger your audience's emotions and truly grab their attention.

The Art of Crafting Compelling Messages

Copywriting is the art of conveying your message to the right people in the most intriguing way. In this chapter, we'll explore the secrets that make words so potent. You'll learn how to craft headlines and subheadings that captivate, influence, and resonate with your audience.

1. The AIDA Model: Crafting Compelling Messages

A cornerstone of copywriting is the **AIDA model**:

- **Attention**: First, grab the reader's attention with a striking headline or opening line.
- **Interest**: Next, spark their interest by addressing their needs or problems.
- **Desire**: Then, build desire by highlighting the benefits and positive outcomes of what you're offering.
- **Action**: Finally, encourage action with a clear and compelling call to action.

By utilizing the AIDA model, you craft communications that effectively lead your audience from initial curiosity to taking meaningful action.

2. Grabbing Attention with Powerful Headlines

Headlines are the **advertisement of the advertisement**. They are responsible for 80% of the success. Headlines and subheadings are the first impression of your message! You need to grab the attention of your potential reader within 2-3 seconds. There are three rules you want to follow when writing headlines:

- Directly Address Your Target Audience
- State the Immediate Benefits of Your Product or Service
- Be Very Specific

Example of a Great Headline:

"Every Lawyer [Audience] Can Triple Their Revenue [Benefit] in 90 Days [Specific]."

Top 5 Most Impactful and Commonly Used Headline Types

When it comes to crafting headlines that capture attention and motivate readers to engage with your content, certain types stand out due to their effectiveness and widespread use. Here are the top five headline types you should focus on:

1. How-To Headlines

- **Purpose**: Offer a solution or teach the reader something valuable.
- **Example**: "How to Unlock Your Full Potential in Just 30 Days"
- **Why It's Effective**: How-to headlines directly address the reader's desire to learn, improve, or solve a problem. They promise clear benefits and practical guidance, making them highly engaging.

2. List Headlines

- **Purpose**: Present information in an easily digestible list format.
- **Example**: "10 Proven Strategies to Boost Your Productivity"
- **Why It's Effective**: Lists are appealing because they organize information into manageable chunks. They set clear expectations about the content and suggest quick, actionable insights.

3. Question Headlines

- **Purpose**: Engage readers by asking a question that resonates with their needs or curiosities.
- **Example**: "Are You Making These Common Mistakes That Sabotage Success?"
- **Why It's Effective**: Questions provoke thought and invite readers to reflect on their own experiences. They create a conversational tone and encourage readers to seek answers by reading further.

4. Benefit Headlines

- **Purpose**: Highlight the main advantage or positive outcome for the reader.
- **Example**: "Achieve Financial Freedom While Doing What You Love"
- **Why It's Effective**: Benefit headlines focus on what the reader stands to gain, tapping directly into their desires and motivations. By showcasing a clear benefit, you provide a compelling reason for them to engage with your content.

5. Curiosity Headlines

- **Purpose**: Spark curiosity by hinting at something intriguing or unexpected.
- **Example**: "The One Secret Successful Entrepreneurs Don't Want You to Know"
- **Why It's Effective**: Curiosity headlines pique interest by creating a sense of mystery or promising insider knowledge. They compel readers to find out more to satisfy their curiosity.

Explain Your Art

While living in Buenos Aires, I helped many tango teachers live their passion and prosper by doing what they love. They used to come to me, the guy in the suit, with big smiles and excitement, totally in love with their product: "online classes." I would take a sip of my Malbec and tell them something that made their smiles disappear.

"My friends," I said, "There are so many tango teachers out there offering classes online. There are a lot of milonga and festival organizers, dance school owners, singers, composers, painters, and tango shops fighting for the attention of potential customers.

But there is only one YOU. So when I say, explain YOUR art, I mean precisely that.

What are you really offering?

A generic description of your offerings will limit your success. You'll only attract the people who already know and appreciate what you do. Doing that is a safe way to lose 99.99% of your income potential. It will also increase your cost of acquiring new customers.

An Exercise to Define Your Unique Value

I asked them to try this exercise—and you should too:

Imagine you're in a room with a thousand other tango lovers whom you've never met before. Besides you, there are ten other people selling a similar product—let's say, "tango classes online." Each seller gets ten seconds per person to convince as many people as possible to buy their product. Each person in the room has money to buy five classes. How many people do you think will buy your product after 20 minutes? And why? What happens if all ten sellers just say, "Tango classes online from beginners to performance"?

Don't worry, I never sent people back without a bigger smile than the one they came in with. Once people really connect and understand the uniqueness of the value they can provide, it clicks. And it works. And it makes money.

Try it with your product. Write down ideas on how you would describe the value you provide to a stranger in 10 seconds.

Copywriting Is the Foundation of Marketing

Words are energy; they trigger emotions and inspire action. The right words can secure the deal you've always dreamed of and open countless doors of opportunity. Conversely, misusing words can evoke unintended emotions, causing you to lose not only opportunities but also friends and valuable connections. Understanding the power of words and harnessing them to achieve your goals is a critical skill you need to master.

Closing Thoughts

In this chapter, we've explored the art of crafting compelling messages that resonate with your audience. By understanding and applying techniques like the AIDA model and mastering the use of powerful headlines, you can elevate your communication and marketing efforts to new heights.

Remember, the key is to **stand out** by being authentically you. Explain your art in a way that highlights your unique value. Use words that not only inform but also inspire and engage. As you refine your copywriting skills, you'll find that opportunities begin to unfold, and your ability to prosper by doing what you love becomes a reality.

Note: A link to the complete copywriter's secret cheat sheet is provided in Chapter 15.

Reflection notes

ACTIONS TO TAKE

-
-
-
-
-
-

IDEAS

-
-
-
-
-
-
-
-
-
-
-
-

ILLUSTRATION

Draw here the first visualization that comes to mind:

GRATITUDE

PERSONAL NOTES

Reflection notes

ACTIONS TO TAKE

-
-
-
-
-
-

IDEAS

-
-
-
-
-
-
-
-
-
-
-
-

ILLUSTRATION

Draw here the first visualization that comes to mind:

GRATITUDE

PERSONAL NOTES

CHAPTER 11

SEDUCING A STRANGER

Falling in Love with Sales and Marketing

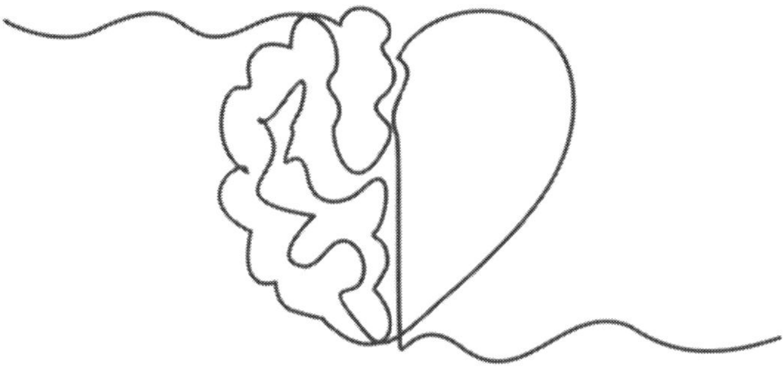

Most people shy away from the sales and marketing aspects of their business. But you're going to love it! You'll become so captivating that people will want to engage with you and gladly pay for the value you provide. When I ask entrepreneurs at my lectures how they plan to attract paying customers for their products, I often receive the same responses:

"What's the problem? We'll use SEO, Facebook Ads, Google Ads, email marketing, and other platforms."

But here's the catch:

If everyone is using the same channels, how will you set yourself apart?

Remember our earlier exercise with the thousand tango lovers in a room? Simply investing more money isn't a sustainable strategy. It operates on the flawed premise that the product's quality is irrelevant—that if someone has a cheap imitation of your product but a bigger budget, they'll always outperform you.

At this point, you might wonder: "Okay, so what if I hire a digital marketing agency to bring me paying clients?"

Delegating your product promotion to an agency is worth considering, but there's a crucial point to remember:

What is the primary goal of digital agencies? Their business is to make money by promoting other people's products or brands. Now, imagine you and your competitor are both clients of the same agency!

Once again, you're faced with the same challenge. The one who pays more gets more attention. Digital marketing agencies work with a diverse range of clients; they don't specialize in your business. It's up to you to differentiate your brand and showcase what makes it valuable to your customers.

So, you might ask: "What can I do to attract more paying customers?"

By now, you understand that promoting generic products or mimicking others won't get you far. Platforms like Facebook and Google are merely vehicles to deliver your message—they're not magic solutions that automatically bring paying customers to your door.

They get paid to display your message; you get paid when someone buys your product.

There are countless marketing services promising to deliver traffic, visitors, and links at the click of a button. While some may offer short-term results, relying solely on them often benefits the service providers more than you. If your competitors use the same services, any advantage diminishes, leaving you back at square one.

The Art of Seducing a Stranger

When I think of sales and marketing, I envision **the art of seducing a stranger**.

Imagine you're at a social gathering and want to connect with someone new. You wouldn't walk up and immediately propose a deep commitment. Instead, you'd aim to grab their attention, be interesting, and present yourself as someone worth getting to know.

Sales and marketing operate on the same principle. You don't start by pushing your highest-priced product. Instead, you offer value—again and again. You allow people to get to know and trust you. You solve a significant part of their problem and then offer a follow-up solution.

In marketing terms, this approach involves **funnels**, **upsells**, and **cross-sells**.

Sales and marketing are the most critical parts of your business. We've prepared comprehensive templates in our Mastermind training to guide you through this process. Please refer to Chapter 15 for access to these resources and follow in the footsteps of many successful people who have made fortunes doing what they love.

Powerful Rules of Marketing

1. Win the Pixel Before You Try to Grab the Whole Picture

Focus on being as specific as possible with your product description and value proposition for your very specific target audience. This precision will increase your conversion rates and reduce advertising costs.

2. Tell Them What They Want to Hear; Give Them What They Need

Use compelling headlines and messages that address the problems your audience faces and how your solution benefits them. Keep your communication focused, clear, and simple. Concentrate on your specific "pixel" in the market.

3. Shift from Selling to Helping

You're not selling unnecessary items; you're providing the right people with the right solutions to their problems. If you have a valuable solution and don't offer it, it's a lose-lose situation—they don't get their problem solved, and you don't get paid.

4. You Are Not Your Product

When someone says "no," they're not rejecting you personally. They might not perceive the value as worth the price. In such cases, provide irresistible value upfront and guide them to more significant offerings as they move through your sales funnel.

5. You Don't Have to Become an Online Marketing Expert

While you can hire an agency to handle your marketing, you cannot delegate your competitive edge, unique features, or value proposition. You're not selling a generic product; you're offering specific, helpful value. It's your responsibility to identify and articulate this value, even if someone else handles the marketing execution.

Determining Your Magic Product Price

You might wonder: "How much should I charge for my product?"

The answer depends on how much you want to earn and, importantly, your advertising dynamics.

For example, let's say you aim to make **$10,000 a month**. If you price your product at **$5**, you'd need **2,000 paying customers** each month. If you price it at **$20**, you'd need only **500 paying customers**.

Which scenario seems more achievable for your product and target audience?

But let's delve deeper into a more powerful concept:

Understanding Customer Acquisition Cost

Calculating how much it costs to acquire a paying customer is crucial. A simple way is to divide your advertising budget by the number of customers gained.

Suppose you spend **$1,000** on Facebook Ads and earn **$1,500** in revenue. This means that for every **$1.00** you invest in ads, you receive **$1.50** in return at a given price point.

The next step is to find the price level that maximizes your return on investment (ROI). This isn't an emotional decision; it's about optimizing dollars and cents.

Here's the exciting part: If you consistently earn **$1.50** for every **$1.00** spent, what's stopping you from scaling up your investment to **$10,000**, **$100,000**, or even **$1,000,000**?

This is how many successful entrepreneurs achieve substantial growth. If you reach this position and need more capital to invest, consider seeking partnerships or investors who can help you scale.

Remember, it's vital to follow the earlier steps correctly. Skipping them can significantly increase your advertising costs. The more generic your product, the more expensive it becomes to attract the right customers. **There are no shortcuts, my friends!**

Marketing: A Complex Yet Seductive Art

Marketing is a multifaceted discipline. It's the art of making a stranger understand your offer in a brief moment, trust you, invest time to get to know you, and ultimately make a purchase.

But here's the good news: **If you master this art, your business will flourish.** You'll have the ability to transform any product or service into a source of life-changing income.

You can enlist the help of experts—see the last chapter of this book for a list of trusted professionals. Alternatively, you can join our Mastermind seminars to gain the knowledge and skills to handle it yourself.

Regardless of the path you choose, remember: **When you leave people happy and satisfied, with a little appetite for more, they will always return and be eager to invest in what you offer.**

Closing Thoughts

Falling in love with sales and marketing transforms how you approach your business. By viewing it as an opportunity to **seduce strangers**—to captivate, engage, and provide genuine value—you shift from merely selling to building lasting relationships.

Embrace the strategies outlined in this chapter:

- **Differentiate Yourself:** Stand out by highlighting what makes you unique.
- **Focus on Value:** Concentrate on solving problems and meeting the needs of your specific audience.
- **Optimize Pricing and Investment:** Understand your numbers to scale effectively.
- **Master the Art:** Continuously refine your marketing skills or collaborate with those who excel in this area.

By doing so, you'll not only attract more paying customers but also create a sustainable and fulfilling business that prospers by doing what you love.

Next Steps:

- Reflect on how you can apply these principles to your own product or service.
- Consider joining our Mastermind seminars for deeper insights.

- Consult Chapter 15 for resources and templates to enhance your marketing efforts.

Let's continue this exciting journey toward success together!

Reflection notes

ACTIONS TO TAKE

-
-
-
-
-
-

IDEAS

-
-
-
-
-
-
-
-
-
-
-
-

ILLUSTRATION

Draw here the first visualization that comes to mind:

GRATITUDE

PERSONAL NOTES

Reflection notes

ACTIONS TO TAKE

-
-
-
-
-
-

IDEAS

-
-
-
-
-
-
-
-
-
-
-
-

ILLUSTRATION

Draw here the first visualization that comes to mind:

GRATITUDE

PERSONAL NOTES

CHAPTER 12

MEET YOUR BRAVE AI ADVANTAGE

Supercharge your advantage with ready-to-use AI prompt

"The saddest aspect of life right now is that science gathers knowledge faster than society gathers wisdom."

Isaac Asimov, 1988

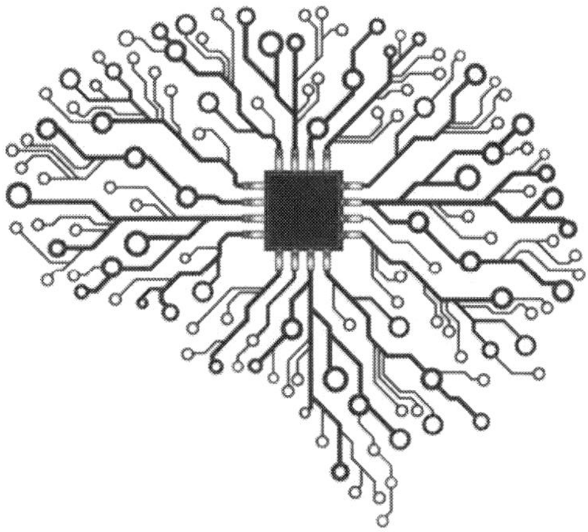

If someone gave you a gift that costs them billions of dollars, completely free, would you be willing to accept it? No obligations. No prerequisites. Just take it as it is.

That's the question facing the world today, as companies like OpenAI, Meta, and Google release powerful artificial intelligence engines for free to anyone who wants them. The immediate question many people ask is, **why?**

Why do these companies give billion-dollar AI models away for free? And since there's no such thing as a free lunch, how much will we pay in the end, and in what way?

As intriguing as these questions are, for the purpose of our journey, they're the wrong ones to ask. Whether you love or hate artificial intelligence, it doesn't matter. **It's here, it's gaining power, and it's a major game changer.**

So, the right question we need to ask is: **How can we use this power for our benefit, today?**

Harnessing the Power of AI

AI has fundamentally changed our world—from one where finding information was a challenge to one where information is abundant and readily accessible. The key now is to harness this wealth of information effectively.

Imagine having someone available 24/7, with access to the universe's information, who can help you create presentations, write marketing plans, brainstorm ideas, or even produce videos. This special assistant never asks for vacations or sick days and never tells you they're too tired to work. In fact, it won't let emotions get in the way and can provide a global perspective on any topic you choose. **How much would you pay to have such an effective assistant?**

Let me introduce you to **GPT** and **Prompts**. The two building blocks of communicating with the machine.

What Is GPT?

GPT (Generative Pre-trained Transformer) is an advanced AI language model developed to understand and generate human-like text based on the input it receives. Think of it as a smart assistant that helps you access the power of vast computational resources through simple human language, written as prompts.

Understanding Prompts

Prompts are the instructions or questions you give to GPT to guide its responses. The clearer and more specific your prompt, the better the AI can assist you. By effectively communicating what you need, you can leverage GPT to help create presentations, marketing plans, brainstorm ideas, and more—all to turn your passion into a thriving business. But, instead of learning the theory, let's look at some real-world examples you can use for your business today.

Five Powerful Prompt Examples to Gain a Positional Advantage Using GPT

Let's explore how you can use GPT to enhance your business endeavours.

1. Creating a Presentation

- **Topic**: Developing a compelling presentation for potential investors.
- **Short Description**: You want to pitch your passion-driven business idea and need help crafting a persuasive presentation that highlights your vision, value proposition, and plans for success.

Prompt Example:

"I'm preparing a 10-slide presentation to pitch my new eco-friendly skincare startup to potential investors. Can you help me outline the key points for each slide, including the problem we're addressing, our unique solutions, target market, competitive advantage, business model, marketing strategy, financial projections, and the team behind the project?"

2. Writing a Short Marketing Plan

- **Topic**: Crafting a marketing plan to launch your business effectively.
- **Short Description**: You need to develop a concise marketing strategy that identifies your target audience and outlines how to reach them.

Prompt Example:

"I am launching an online handmade jewellery store called "Malena Gems,' targeting women aged 25-40 who appreciate artisanal accessories. Could you help me write a short marketing plan that includes identifying my target audience, key marketing channels (like Instagram and Pinterest), content ideas, promotional strategies, and a brief budget outline?"

3. Brainstorming Business Ideas

- **Topic**: Generating innovative ideas to expand your passion into new opportunities.

- **Short Description**: You're seeking creative ways to grow your business or diversify your offerings.

Prompt Example:

"My passion is baking artisan bread, and I currently run a small bakery. I want to expand my business. Can you help me brainstorm ideas for new products, services, or experiences that align with my passion and could attract more customers?"

4. Planning Social Media Content

- **Topic**: Developing engaging content for your social media platforms.
- **Short Description**: You aim to build a strong online presence to connect with your audience and promote your business.

Prompt Example:

"I own a fitness coaching business called 'Super Gracie' that offers personalized training programs. Can you help me create a month's worth of social media content ideas for Instagram and Facebook? I'd like to include fitness tips, client success stories, motivational quotes, and promotional offers."

5. Crafting a Mission Statement

- **Topic**: Defining the core purpose and values of your business.
- **Short Description**: You need assistance articulating a mission statement that reflects your passion and guides your business decisions.

Prompt Example:

"I'm starting an eco-friendly clothing line named 'Green Things' that uses sustainable materials and ethical manufacturing practices. Could you help me craft a compelling mission statement that conveys our commitment to the environment, sustainability, and ethical fashion?"

Powerful isn't it? Think how much time and research your new AI assistant can save you. Learning and integrating this power into your journey will grant you a competitive edge and allow you to trade less of your time for money.

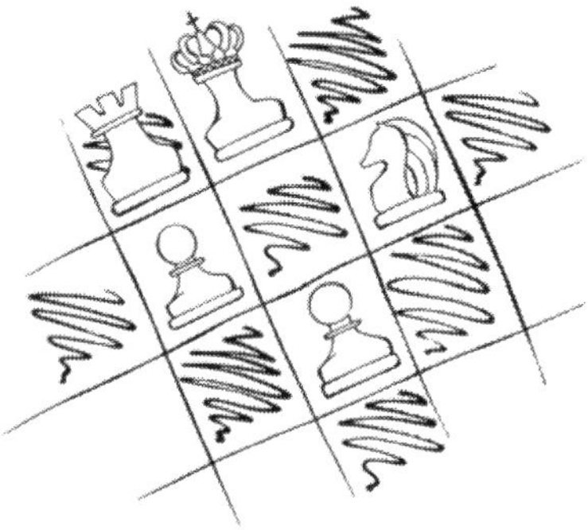

Tips for Effective Prompts

To get the most out of GPT, consider the following tips:

- **Be Specific**: Clearly state what you need and include relevant details.
  - *Instead of*: "Help me with marketing."
  - *Try*: "I need ideas for a social media campaign to promote my new line of organic teas to health-conscious consumers."
- **Provide Context**: Briefly explain your business and goals so GPT can tailor its response.
  - *Include details like*: Your business name, target audience, unique selling points, and any challenges you're facing.
- **Ask Direct Questions or Give Clear Instructions**: This guides GPT to provide focused and useful answers.
  - *Example*: "What are some effective strategies to increase online sales for handmade crafts?"
- **Specify the Desired Format**: If you need bullet points, a summary, or step-by-step instructions, mention it.
  - *Example*: "List five innovative ways to market my photography services locally."

Mastering the Art of GPT Prompts

Don't miss the train, and don't let your emotions about AI keep you behind the curve. Whether you're crafting a presentation, devising a marketing plan, brainstorming new ideas, or defining your mission, GPT can be a valuable ally in turning your passion into a successful source of income.

Remember, the key is to communicate clearly and provide enough information for GPT to generate helpful and relevant responses. With practice, you'll find that GPT can enhance your productivity, creativity, and strategic planning—helping you gain a significant positional advantage on your journey to prosperity.

I've created a GPT cheat sheet to help you boost your success; the link is in Chapter 15.

Closing Thoughts

Artificial intelligence, and GPT in particular, is more than just a technological advancement—it's a tool that can empower you to achieve your goals more efficiently and effectively. By embracing AI, you're not only staying ahead of the curve but also unlocking new possibilities for innovation and growth.

So, take the leap. Start experimenting with GPT. See how it can assist you in your daily tasks, amplify your strengths, and help you overcome challenges. The future is here, and it's brimming with opportunities for those who are willing to embrace change and leverage new tools.

Reflection notes

ACTIONS TO TAKE

-
-
-
-
-
-

IDEAS

-
-
-
-
-
-
-
-
-
-
-
-

ILLUSTRATION

Draw here the first visualization that comes to mind:

GRATITUDE

PERSONAL NOTES

Reflection notes

ACTIONS TO TAKE

-
-
-
-
-
-

IDEAS

-
-
-
-
-
-
-
-
-
-
-
-

ILLUSTRATION

Draw here the first visualization that comes to mind:

GRATITUDE

PERSONAL NOTES

CHAPTER 13

GET INTO THE RING WITH MIKE TYSON

Are You Ready to Jump into the Ring and Win?

In his manifesto, *The Art of War,* Sun Tzu wrote that **if you know yourself and you know your enemy, you should not fear the results of a hundred battles.** In this book, we've covered the "know yourself" part, and we've seen that to defeat a stronger enemy, we need to gather a sequence of positional advantages—and better yet, make it a daily habit.

By now, you should have the tools, strategies, and clarity to get your journey in motion. You're about to jump into the market with the things you love and make a fortune. But let me ask you a quick question:

If you were to step into the ring with Mike Tyson when he was in his prime, do you think you could beat him? Or at least stay alive?

Unless your name is Muhammad Ali, the answer would, of course, be no. But what if you had a winning element that changes the whole position of the game? Maybe, for example, a weapon or a unique fight strategy. Would that change your chances of winning?

Finding Your Winning Element

In every situation, there's often a crucial element that can change everything. Sometimes, it's about adding another component that turns the whole scenario around. We've previously discussed deflection and the joker position. But here, it's about introducing a new element—something that will shift the energy flow.

When you feel stuck or need to jump into the ring with your own "Mike Tyson," you want to find your winning element. What is your winning element?

The marketplace is a tough arena, but it's also vast. You need to choose your battles wisely so you don't exhaust your energy and resources on steps outside your critical path.

You Can't Win from the Sidelines

The truth is—you can't win from the sidelines. You must jump into the ring if you want to win the fight. One of the most common mistakes that prevent people from owning their journey is that they're afraid to jump into the ring. They stay on the sidelines, where there's no commitment and no risk of failure. Most people prefer to watch someone else lose a fight in the ring rather than be there themselves.

But as we've discussed before, in terms of positional advantages, being in the ring is a massive advantage, regardless of the fight's outcome. In life, we encounter many opportunities we avoid because we don't want to face the consequences of jumping into the ring. We let beautiful moments go unfulfilled because we're scared of the potential fallout. We don't approach someone we're interested in because we're afraid of rejection. We skip amazing experiences because we're worried about what others might say about us.

The Story of the Bachata Dancer

Several years ago, I gave a keynote talk at the Founders Institute in Berlin. I spoke about strategies, sharing examples and stories. While discussing the importance of jumping into the ring, a young woman in the audience began to cry.

During the break, we shared a glass of wine, and I asked her what had happened. She told me that all her life, she had been afraid to jump into the ring and was saddened by all the opportunities and moments she had missed. She was a professional bachata dancer. I invited her to one of my workshops, and our paths parted after that. I didn't hear from her for a long time.

One Friday, I was sitting at a café having breakfast when someone approached me, gave me a warm hug, and said thank you. It was the bachata dancer, and she was crying again—but this time, they were tears of happiness.

She told me that my workshop had helped her find the courage to jump into the ring. She had accepted a very minor role at the opera in Berlin. In fact, it wasn't dancing or singing—just standing there in the background, adding beauty to the overall composition.

This was something she would never have done before, as she feared her colleagues and other dancers would make fun of her. But she did it. She stood there proudly, playing her role.

Unlike most of her colleagues, she was in the ring. She was in the game. Stepping into the ring was such an important step for her. People who never do it—because the role isn't fancy enough, they're afraid of what others might say, or they lack the courage—are not going to win.

And now, she had secured a much bigger contract. She joined me for breakfast and told me about her journey and transformation. It made me incredibly happy. My passion is to help others prosper in things that make their hearts rumble.

Embrace the Opportunity

So, are you going to jump into the ring the next time an opportunity unfolds?

Stepping into the ring is a decision to engage with life fully. It's about embracing opportunities, facing challenges head-on, and not letting fear dictate your actions. Whether it's starting a new business, pursuing a passion, or taking on a role that pushes your boundaries, being in the ring means you're in the game.

Remember, you can't win from the sidelines. The ring is where growth happens, where lessons are learned, and where victories are earned. It's not about guaranteed success; it's about giving yourself the chance to succeed.

Identifying Your Winning Element

As you prepare to jump into the ring, consider what your winning element might be. What unique advantage can you bring to the situation that changes the game in your favour?

- **Is it a specific skill or talent you possess?**
- **Do you have a unique perspective or approach that others lack?**
- **Can you leverage relationships or networks to enhance your position?**
- **Are there tools or resources you can use to shift the dynamics?**

Identifying and utilizing your winning element can make all the difference when facing formidable challenges.

Someday, someone will say something that triggers powerful thoughts in you. You need to be open to that! Often, these thoughts will become your greatest edge and perhaps your best next move. Remember the Opportunity Magnet chapter? Well, you should not only be ready to act upon those triggers but also always try to give others this gift.

Closing Thoughts

Life is full of rings—arenas where battles are fought, challenges are faced, and opportunities await. Whether it's the marketplace, personal relationships, or personal growth, the principle remains the same: you must step into the ring to win.

Don't let fear hold you back. Embrace the journey, take calculated risks, and remember that being in the game is itself a significant advantage. Even if you don't win every battle, the experience, growth, and potential for success far outweigh the safety of the sidelines.

So, are you ready to jump into the ring and win?

Reflection notes

ACTIONS TO TAKE

-
-
-
-
-
-

IDEAS

-
-
-
-
-
-
-
-
-
-
-
-

ILLUSTRATION

Draw here the first visualization that comes to mind:

GRATITUDE

PERSONAL NOTES

Reflection notes

ACTIONS TO TAKE

IDEAS

ILLUSTRATION

Draw here the first visualization that comes to mind:

GRATITUDE

PERSONAL NOTES

PART 3

The Way Forward and Bonuses

CHAPTER 14

CROSSING YOUR NEXT INVISIBLE BRIDGE

United by a Life-Changing Journey—Forward and Onward

She gazed into the mirror, a radiant smile spreading across her face, and whispered softly to herself:

"This time, we did things differently. We laughed more. We loved more. We didn't waste our days merely working—we embraced the world with open arms. Fear no longer held us captive. I remember when I used to keep my head down, hustling just to get through life, saving some money but missing so much. Then one day, I looked up and asked, how did I even get here?

So we took that first step across the invisible bridge. We created our own path, found clarity, and made our best moves. We turned obstacles into opportunities and passions into prosperity. We've seen places that took our breath away, met people who touched our hearts, and did work that truly mattered to us.

Now, there are no regrets—only a heart full of joy and a life rich with experiences. We kept learning, kept growing, and every day became an adventure worth living. We've lived our passion, and it feels incredible."

We Are Approaching the Final Station

We are nearing the last stop of this book, where your personal journey truly begins. I hope the insights shared here have inspired you to make your heart rumble again and to follow your passion. This is not a goodbye; it's a heartfelt good luck. I'm excited and happy for everyone who has come this far. The knowledge and strategies you've gained are a treasure, and the value of this treasure expands as you continue on your journey.

Let's Review Some Key Points

I hope your "personal actions" list is ready and that you're already crossing some bridges that were previously invisible to you. Let's revisit some important points we've discussed along the way:

- **Finish What You Start**

  World-class achievers develop the habit of seeing things through to completion. Quitting can easily become a bad habit, and we already know how hard it is to change one. Remember this basic truth: you need to get things done. The way you do anything is the way you do everything. So, do it with your heart—do it properly.

- **Don't Just Do It—Own It**

  People often wonder how I can accomplish so much so thoroughly. The reason is simple: when I do something, I own it. I'm not just doing it because someone told me to; I take full responsibility and invest myself completely. If you want to achieve great things, you need to own your tasks, whether it's a small assignment or a multimillion-dollar project. Master the execution and own the process.

- **Be Responsible for Everything**

  Embrace this mindset: *"It is not my fault, but I am responsible."* Even when things are beyond your control, taking responsibility empowers you. Blaming others creates a weak position and takes control out of your hands.

What Wine Should We Open to Celebrate Your Win?

Now, it's time to celebrate! You've achieved a significant milestone by finishing this book, and I'm so happy for you. But what wine should we open?

This is a question I often receive. Everywhere I go, people ask me, *"**What is your favourite wine?**"* Before we part ways, let me share one last story that carries a strong lesson.

When I went to the south of France to take my advanced WSET wine exam, I tried to answer this question myself: What is my favourite wine? After travelling the world for many years, living and working in different countries, and building international businesses, I couldn't find the answer in the technicalities of wine tasting. Instead, I arrived at an answer that has served me well to this day.

My favourite wine is one that leaves a memorable impression on me. It's a wine that impacts me and enhances the moment I'm in. It's part of a story—a story of friendship, love, business, origin, or nostalgia.

Have you ever heard someone excitedly tell you about a small restaurant in the south of Italy that served the best cola they've ever had? Probably not. That's because cola doesn't create an unforgettable impression. Sugar is sugar, wherever you go. Similarly, many wines are as generic as cola. But some make you want to run and share your amazing experience with others. Those are my favourite wines.

For the purpose of this book, remember that you don't want to be perceived as a can of cola. You want to be the amazing wine that impacts moments in a memorable way, creating experiences people want to embrace.

I know this book will take you on a beautiful journey. So, if you come across an amazing wine that shapes your experience in a meaningful way, please share! Send me the details—or better yet, the bottle—and I'll share it with our community.

You Are Not Alone—It's Your Time to Shine

Many amazing people around the world are benefiting from the insights in this book. Just like you, they are embracing powerful ideas, creating positional advantages, building winning habits, and living the lives they deserve.

I won't leave you to navigate this journey by yourself. My mission is to help millions prosper by doing what they love and to experience life more fully. It's important to surround yourself with people who inspire, motivate, and support you—like-minded individuals who refuse to settle for the daily grind.

You might wonder what others who have completed this book are doing now. Where are they from? What were their next steps? You already feel connected to these readers you haven't met yet—strangers united by a life-changing journey.

These strangers can become your friends, and together, you can change the world.

Join our community of readers here:

www.CrossingTheInvisibleBridge.com/together

Are You Ready to Make Money Helping Others?

If you loved this book and are already feeling your heart rumble with excitement for the journey ahead, let's help more people together. Share the book with your friends; help them prosper and be happier. They'll receive a **20% discount**, and you'll get **$10** for every friend who buys the book.

Register here to get your personal discount codes:

www.CrossingTheInvisibleBridge.com/friends-affiliate

Closing Thoughts

This is your move. The invisible bridge is before you, waiting for you to take that first step. You've gathered the knowledge, honed your strategies, and ignited your passion. Now, it's time to cross over into the life you've envisioned.

Remember, the journey doesn't end here—it begins. Embrace it fully, live your passion, and let your heart rumble with the excitement of new possibilities.

Here's to you—to your courage, your dreams, and the incredible journey ahead.

Cheers!

Reflection notes

ACTIONS TO TAKE

-
-
-
-
-
-

IDEAS

-
-
-
-
-
-
-
-
-
-
-
-

ILLUSTRATION

Draw here the first visualization that comes to mind:

GRATITUDE

PERSONAL NOTES

Reflection notes

ACTIONS TO TAKE

-
-
-
-
-
-

IDEAS

-
-
-
-
-
-
-
-
-
-
-
-

ILLUSTRATION

Draw here the first visualization that comes to mind:

GRATITUDE

PERSONAL NOTES

CHAPTER 15

NEXT STEPS AND BONUSES

Next Steps, Bonuses, make money offer and great companies

Don't Get Left Behind! Join Our Global Community Today

Are you ready to connect with like-minded individuals determined to support each other on the path to prosperity, passion, and happiness? When you register, you'll gain access to our exclusive Platinum Club bonuses:

- **Copywriting Secrets Cheat Sheet**
- **Powerful Marketing Plan Template**
- **AI GPT–Ready-to-Use Expert Prompts**
- **My Personal Health Protocol**
- **My Personal 10x Efficiency Protocol**
- **Financial vehicles I personally use to make 20%-70% on my money every year.**

*Total Value: $1,765—**FREE** for the first 10,000 book readers!*

☞ **Register now at:**

www.CrossingTheInvisibleBridge.com/together

Exclusive 1:1 Strategy Call with Ofer Valencio Akerman

This is a rare opportunity available only to readers committed to generating substantial income by doing what they love. I invite you to schedule a personal Strategy Call with me, lasting 30 to 45 minutes in a one-on-one setting. This session is highly impactful, so please arrange it only when you are fully prepared to take the next step.

Book your Strategy Call here:
www.CrossingTheInvisibleBridge.com/strategy-call

Use Bonus Code: Book70 *(Get 70% Discount) Only **500** calls available—don't miss out!*

Make Money by Helping Others

Are You Ready to Earn While Making a Difference?

If you loved this book and feel your heart rumbling with excitement for the journey ahead, let's help more people together. Share the book with your friends; help them prosper and be happier. They'll receive a **20% discount**, and you'll get **$10** for every friend who buys the book.

Register here and start earning by helping others:
www.CrossingTheInvisibleBridge.com/friends-affiliate

Your Next Move Awaits

Don't let this moment pass you by. Whether it's accessing valuable resources, getting personalized guidance, or seizing opportunities to help others and grow your income, the time to act is now.

Remember, prosperity isn't just about wealth—it's about living a life filled with passion, clarity, and fulfilment. You've already taken the first step by reading this book. Now, let's continue this journey together.

See you on the other side of the bridge!

Your Personal Actions List

Note your thoughts, ideas and actions here

TOP PRIORITY - ACTIONS TO TAKE

-
-
-
-
-
-

IDEAS

-
-
-
-
-
-
-
-
-
-
-
-

ILLUSTRATION

GRATITUDE

OPEN LOOPS TO ELIMINATE OR FULLY ACCEPT

Printed in Great Britain
by Amazon

e545f7c8-4ef8-442b-a5f1-623fea3d4348R01